You
Are
Chosen

You
Are
Chosen

The Priesthood of
All Believers

Herschel H. Hobbs

1817

Harper & Row, Publishers, San Francisco

New York, Grand Rapids, Philadelphia, St. Louis
London, Singapore, Sydney, Tokyo, Toronto

YOU ARE CHOSEN: *The Priesthood of All Believers.* Copyright © 1990 by Herschel H. Hobbs. All rights reserved. Printed in the United States of America. No part of this book may be used or reproduced in any manner whatsoever without written permission except in the case of brief quotations embodied in critical articles and reviews. For information address Harper & Row, Publishers, Inc., 10 East 53rd Street, New York, NY 10022.

FIRST EDITION

Library of Congress Cataloging-In-Publication Data
Hobbs, Herschel H.
    You are chosen : the priesthood of all believers / Herschel H.
  Hobbs. — 1st ed.
      p.   cm.
  Includes bibliographical references.
  ISBN 0-06-252004-0
  1. Priesthood, Universal. 2. Christian life—Baptist authors.
I. Title.
BT767.5.H63 1990
234—dc20   89-45183
                                                 CIP

90 91 92 93 94 HAD 10 9 8 7 6 5 4 3 2 1

Dedicated to
All Believers
Who Honor Their Priesthood

Contents

Preface

In Christian circles around the world there is an aroused interest in the doctrine of the priesthood of the believer. This is coupled with renewed interest throughout all the church community in the relationship between the clergy and laity. At the same time, voices in my own fellowship, the Southern Baptist Convention, are calling for pastoral authority.

Even in those churches that accept the doctrine of the priesthood of the believer there are diverse understandings of its exact meaning. For instance, does this teaching involve privilege, or responsibility, or both? How does it relate to salvation, ministry, and church polity? What part does the Holy Spirit play? In a complex social order that calls for ""big government," how does this doctrine relate to religious liberty? And what is the role of the Holy Spirit when this teaching is followed?

Volumes could be written on any one of these factors, but obviously a work of this scope permits only a sketchy treatment. At the same time it is not an apologetic for any particular strain of the Christian faith. Frequent references to Baptists reflect, their historically active and leading role in the struggle for religious freedom.

My purpose here, though, is to be of help to all Christians everywhere who are wrestling with the problems of religious freedom in a complex world.

You
Are
Chosen

1. The Competency of the Soul

Reduced to its simplest form, the principle of the priesthood of all believers means that all believers in Christ are priests. And as will be seen, this vital doctrine colors the whole of Christian relationships. However, before exploring it we must look beyond it to an even broader concept, which is the source of this and other principles relating to various aspects of our spiritual relationships.

A Baptist leader of a past generation posed this important question. "What is the historical significance of the Baptists? What great principle have they contributed to the religious thought and life of mankind? Or to state the question in a slightly different form, What interpretation of Christianity do they represent which distinguishes them from all other Christian bodies?"[1]

In response, we immediately think of certain great principles held by Baptists: salvation by grace through faith; believer's baptism (immersion); regenerated church membership; autonomy of the local church; priesthood of the believer; separation of church and state. However, these can hardly be called distinctly Baptist, because some if not all of them are held by other Christian groups. "All of these are vitally important and grow directly out of Baptists' fundamental position. But they are corollaries to a prior truth. They are not original but derived."[2]

What, then, is this distinctive contribution of Baptists to the Christian world? It is the competency of the soul in religion. This does not mean a competency of human self-sufficiency, but instead it is a competency under God. In the Christian sense it is a Christ-sufficiency. In short, it means that every person, or soul, is competent to stand before God without any need for a human or human-made "go-between." This truth

is clearly seen in the relationship between God and his creation—humankind.

God is the infinite spiritual Person. As such he can not have
fellowship with rocks, trees, planets, or solar systems simply because a spiritual person can have fellowship only with another
of like kind. Early in our Bible we read, "So God created man in
his own image, in the image of God created he him, male and
female created he them" (Gen. 1:27; cf. 2:7).

Since God is Spirit, "image" refers to spiritual, not physical
likeness. So the infinite Person created finite persons. And as
God is Spirit (John 4:24), we his creation, also possess a spiritual
nature. This means we are capable of direct spiritual fellowship
with God.

In addition, we're told that 'God is love" (1 John 4:8), and love
reveals itself. So as Love, God reveals himself to us, to people.
And we are able to receive that revelation. At the same time,
we are endowed with the capacity for choice. But we are also
responsible for the choices we make, and our responsibility is
to God, not to other people. To emphasize this point Paul wrote
to his critics at Corinth, "But with me it is a very small thing that
I should be judged of you, or of man's judgment: yea, I judge not
mine own self. For I know nothing by myself; yet am I not hereby justified: but he that judgeth me is the Lord" (2 Cor. 4:3-4).

Furthermore, as spiritual persons we have a capacity for God.
In fact, as authentic human beings, we can never be satisfied
apart from God. Augustine expressed it well when he said that
God has made us for himself, and our souls are not satisfied until they find rest in him. The Psalmist put it this way, "As the
hart panteth after the water brooks, so panteth my soul after
thee, O God. My soul thirsteth for God, for the living God"
(Ps. 42:1-2). E.Y. Mullins echoes this truth. "Even in the most
wicked of hearts there is an echo of what that person might have
been—what, indeed, in his deeper self he wants to be.[3]

It should be recognized, however, that soul competency does
not mean that people can believe anything they choose and
claim to be a Christian or a Baptist, Methodist, Presbyterian,

Lutheran, or an Episcopalian. It does mean, though, that we can choose to be a Christian, Jew, Muslim, Hindu, agnostic, even an atheist. But we are responsible to God for our choices. Even God does not force us to believe in him. To do so would make us puppets, not persons. And God loves us too much to destroy our personhood.

The principle of soul competency is both exclusive and inclusive.[4] For instance, it excludes human interference of any kind between the individual soul and God. In its deepest sense, religion is a personal matter between the individual and God, and for the soul to be responsible, it must be free. Since our responsibility is to God, this excludes any human interference or barrier between ourselves and God.

On the other hand, soul competency is inclusive. It includes salvation by grace through faith without the need of a human mediator or any institution, ecclesiastical or political.

Institutions, of course, have their place. But they are not to stand in the way of our direct access to God. This does not negate the social aspects of the Christian faith. As individuals we stand face to face with God in Christ, but believers collectively are to cooperate in the achievement of common goals for the benefit of the social order. The gospel is spiritual in nature, but it also has social implications.

Soul competency naturally calls for a regenerated church membership. And this in turn calls for democratic church government at the human level and a Christocratic government at the divine level. It also calls for the separation of church and state. The state has nothing to offer the soul in its eternal destiny.

Also the competency of the soul calls for the priesthood of believers. And as we will see later, this involves both privilege and responsibility.

As was made clear in an earlier book, "the competency of the regenerated individual is derived from the indwelling Christ through the Holy Spirit. Man's capacity in self-government in religion is nothing more or less than the authority of Christ exerted in and through the inner life of the believer—with the understanding always, of course, that he regulates that inner life in accordance with his revealed Word. . . . Democracy in church government is simply Christ himself animating his own body through his Spirit. The decisions of the local congregation on ecclesiastical matters are [as one has called it] 'the consensus of the competent.' "[5]

Happily, most of our late twentieth-century Christian community is in considerable agreement with the principle of the priesthood of the believer. But it will be both revealing and helpful to turn our attention now to an examination of this principle and how it relates to other principles that emerge from the concepts of the competency of the soul in religion.

2. The History of the Priesthood of the Believer

In a work of the scope of this book it is impossible to give an exhaustive study of the history of this important principle. But we can at least sketch its history. Even in the most primitive of religions we find those who functioned in a priestly office, regardless of what they were called. Among the Hebrews (prior to the designation of the tribe of Levi as the priestly tribe, with Aaron, Moses' brother, as the first high priest), the father in each family filled this role. Among other things in those ancient times, he presided at the sacrifice of animals.

Under the Mosaic system, the tribe of Levi was the priestly tribe. Since they gave all their time serving in the tabernacle and later in the Temple, they received no territorial allotment in Canaan but were dependent on the other tribes for their material needs.

The Mosaic Covenant

According to the story, three months, or "moons," after the exodus from Egypt, the Hebrews arrived at Mt. Sinai (Exod. 19:1). There, through Moses, God entered into a covenant with the people of Israel.

After reminding them of all he had done for them, God said, "Now therefore, if ye will obey my voice indeed, and keep my covenant, then ye shall be a peculiar treasure unto me above all people: for all the earth is mine: And ye shall be unto me a kingdom of priests, and an holy nation" (Exod. 19:5—6). The reference here to "a peculiar treasure" is interesting. In ancient times a king was said to own everything in his realm, only allowing the people to use his resources. But the king also had his private collection, such as precious gems, which were for his enjoyment alone. These were his "peculiar [personal] treasure."

Though all the people on earth belonged to God, he stated that the Hebrews were his "peculiar treasure." They were to be a "kingdom of priests" (note the plural), a "holy nation," or one set apart, dedicated to his use. Now a priest was one who stood between God and humans in order to bring them together. And here we're told that the nation of Israel was to fill this role in bringing pagan people to worship and serve the one true God. They were selected for both privilege and service. God chose them, not because he loved them more than other people. But God chose the people of Israel to lead the pagan people to him, and there was both privilege and responsibility in their role.

The key words in Exod. 19:5 are "if" and "then" because this indicates the covenant or agreement was conditional. As a rule in ancient times covenants were made between a greater and lesser party. The greater party set conditions, which must be met by the lesser party. Otherwise, the greater party was not bound by the promises.

We read that the people of Israel agreed to the covenant (Exod. 19:8), and God located them in Canaan, which centuries before he had promised to Abraham and his descendants. Canaan (Palestine) served as a land bridge between the Mediterranean Sea on the west and the Arabian Desert on the east. It joined the three known continents of that time. From it the Hebrews could fan out and influence the pagan nations of the ancient world.

But history records that Israel never fulfilled the conditions of the covenant. Instead of evangelizing the pagan Canaanites, they were paganized by them. Biblical history gives us the sad story of a long line of prophets that were sent to urge the people of Israel to honor the covenant but to no avail.

Following the death of Solomon, the ten northern tribes rebelled and founded the Northern Kingdom of Israel under Jeroboam I. The prophet Amos, under the leadership of the Lord, referred to this as "the sinful kingdom" (Amos 9:8). However, it could also be translated the "illegal" or "unlawful" kingdom.[1] It was not a part of the covenant people, since the Lord's redemptive purpose ran through the tribe of Judah, or the Southern Kingdom of Judah. Because of sin, the Northern Kingdom was conquered by the Assyrians in 722 B.C. The Southern Kingdom of Judah survived until it was laid waste by the Babylonians in 587 B.C. Judah failed to honor the Mosaic Covenant, but instead turned to pagan gods.

The New Covenant

Shortly before the fall of Judah, the Lord announced through the prophet Jeremiah that he would make a new covenant with his people (Jer. 31:31—34). Unlike the old Mosaic Covenant, in the new one the Lord said, "I will put my law in their inward parts [not on tablets of stone], and write it in their hearts. . . . And they shall teach no more every man his neighbor, and every man his brother, saying, Know the Lord: for they shall all know me, from the least of them unto the greatest of them, saith the Lord" (Jer. 31:33—34). And the writer of the book of Hebrews says that this promise was fulfilled in Christ. The new covenant was sealed with his blood (Heb. 9:11—12, 15—28).

In light of the emphasis upon evangelism and missions in the New Testament (Covenant), the words of Jeremiah certainly don't mean that we are not to share the gospel with people who haven't heard it. Among other things, though, it suggests the end of the Levitical priesthood. Under the old covenant, for instance, the people depended upon the priests to determine what sacrifices were required for certain sins, and then the priests made those sacrifices.

Furthermore, in the tabernacle and the Temple only priests could enter the Court of the Priests and into the Holy Place where sacrifices were made. Only the high priest could enter the Holy of Holies where God was said to dwell in mercy with his people. And the high priest could do that only on the annual Day of Atonement.

Non-Jews had access only to the Court of the Gentiles in the Temple. Jewish women were restricted to the Court of the Women. And Jewish men, other than priests, were not permitted beyond the Court of Israel.

According to Jewish custom, a Gentile had no access to God. Only Jews and Jewish proselytes could approach God, and they could do so only through priestly intermediaries. But under the new covenant all believers in Christ have direct access to God through Jesus. This simply means that in the Lord's promise of a new covenant we have the concept of the priesthood of believers in embryo.

The New Priesthood

The time and setting we want to focus on now is Tuesday of Passion Week. It has been referred to as "a day of controversy."[2] Jesus had been preaching and teaching from Galilee to Judea for over three years, and it was clear now that the Jewish religious leaders would not accept him as the Messiah. Jesus knew of their decision to condemn him to death if they could. But to accomplish that the Jewish leaders attempted to discredit him with the people (Matt. 21:23—23:29) by challenging his cleansing of the Temple and his authority to teach (see Matt. 21:23—32).

In response to their challenge Jesus told the story of the evil tenant vine-growers (Matt. 21:33—41). According to the story a certain landowner planted a vineyard and then, because he was going to be out of the country, he leased it out to tenants. In due course, the landowner sent some of his servants to collect the rent, but the tenants refused to pay and they beat some of the servants and killed others. Next the landowner sent more servants, and they met with the same fate as the first group. Finally, the landowner sent his son, but the wicked tenants killed him and threw his body out of the vineyard.

After telling this story Jesus asked the Jewish leaders what the landowner should do to the rebellious tenants. Their reply was direct and to the point, "He will miserably destroy those wicked men, and will let his vineyard out unto other husbandmen [tenants], which shall render him the fruits in their season [who would pay the rent]" (Matt. 21:41).

Now, in this story we understand that the vineyard represents the nation of Israel. We believe, too, that the servants sent to collect the rent represent the prophets who attempted to get the people of Israel to honor their covenant with the Lord, which they never did. Finally, the son that was sent obviously represented Jesus, whom the Jewish leaders rejected and wanted to kill.

Next, the writer of Matthew tells us that when Jesus heard their stern condemnation, he said to them, "Did ye never read in the scriptures, 'The stone which the builders rejected, the same is become the head of the corner: this is the Lord's doing, and it is marvelous in our eyes?' Therefore say I unto you, The kingdom of God shall be taken from you, and given to a nation bringing forth the fruits thereof. And whatsoever shall fall on this stone shall be broken: but on whomsoever it shall fall, it will grind him to powder" (Matt. 21:42—44).

It was then, the writer of Matthew tells us, that the Jewish religious leaders understood that he was speaking about them–their rejection and evil intent. And just forty years later (A.D. 70) the invading Roman armies crushed the Jewish nation, and they never again occupied a place of importance in the religious sphere.

In this encounter on that fateful Tuesday Jesus definitely sounded the death knell to Israel's covenant relationship with the Lord God. Because Israel failed to meet the *condition*, God was not bound by the *promise* (cf. Exod. 19:5—6). And while God still loves the Jewish people and longs to save them in Jesus Christ, that is quite separate from the old Mosaic Covenant.

Now, to round out the picture, let us examine the message in 1 Pet. 2:1—10. By way of summary there, the writer speaks of the "new priesthood." Comparing these words with Exod. 19:5—6 and Matt. 21:42—44, it seems that Peter deliberately combined the language of these passages to show his Christian readers, and all others like them, that they are "a chosen generation, a royal priesthood, an holy nation, a peculiar people, that ye should shew forth the praises of him who hath called you out of darkness into his marvelous light: which in time past were not a people [constituted nation], but are now the people of God: which had not obtained mercy, but now have obtained mercy" (1 Peter 2:9—10).

Thus the covenant people of God are Jews, and Gentiles, regardless of race or ethnic group, who have received Jesus Christ as Savior and Lord. We, then, are the new kingdom of priests, a people dedicated to proclaiming the gospel to a lost world.

New Testament Priesthood

When we turn to the New Testament we sense an atmosphere of freedom. Of course, we still find the Levitical priesthood, but it was confined to Judaism. However, in dealing with the new covenant in contrast to the old, the author of Hebrews says, "In that he [God] saith, A new covenant, he hath made the first old. Now that which decayeth and waxeth old is ready to vanish away [or disappear] (Heb. 8:13).

These words in both Hebrews and 1 Peter were probably written shortly before A.D. 70. This date marked the destruction of Jerusalem and its Temple. With it also went the old order, including its priestly and sacrificial system. There has been no animal sacrifice in Judaism since that time.

The New Testament emphasis is upon a new order of priests and priesthood. With few exceptions these words may sound strange to our ears, but they are used in the New Testament in the Christian sense (1 Pet. 2:5, 9; Rev. 1:5—6; 5:9—10; 20:6). In addition, the concept of the priesthood of believers is found in places where thee words are not used.

The principle of the priesthood of believers has its roots in the high priesthood of Christ. He is Prophet, Priest, and King;

a truth expressed in Heb. 1:1—3. As prophet, Christ is God's complete, final revelation to humankind. As priest, he "himself purged our sins." As king, he "sat down on the right hand of the Majesty on high."[3] Biblical prophecy points to the time when he will be "King of Kings, and Lord of Lords" (Rev. 19:16).

One of the key words in Hebrews is "better." In Christ we have a *better* revelation, a *better* high priest, a *better* tabernacle, a *better* covenant, and a *better* sacrifice.

As for the better high priesthood, the author of Hebrews compares Christ with Aaron whose office had a definite beginning and end. The writer says that, unlike Aaron, Christ's priestly office is eternal. Quoting from Ps. 110:4, a messianic psalm, he says, "Thou art a priest for ever after the order of Melchizedek" (cf. Heb. 5:6, 10; 6:20; 7:7, 12, 21). And Melchizedek is described as "without father, without mother, without descent [genealogy], having neither beginning of days, nor end of life; but made like unto the Son of God: abideth a priest continually" (Heb. 7:3).

Other than in Psalms and Hebrews, Melchizedek is mentioned only in Genesis 14. Nothing is said about his parents, birth, death, or genealogy. In a sense he is timeless insofar as the record shows. The author of Hebrews draws upon this fact to show the nature of Christ's high priesthood. It is his way of saying it is eternal.

Even though Christ's priesthood is eternal, he manifested himself in time (John 1:1, 14). Consequently, "we have not an high priest which cannot be touched with the feeling of our infirmities, but was in all points tempted like as we are, yet without sin" (Heb. 4:15). And Christ became both priest and sacrifice as he died to provide salvation for all who believe in him.

As has previously been stated, our priesthood grows out of Christ's High Priesthood. In the opening verses of Revelation, John ascribes glory and dominion to him who "loved us, and washed us from our sins in his own blood" and, literally, "made us kings, priests unto God and his Father" (1:5b—6).

We have noted that in the Mosaic covenant (Exod. 19:5—6) God promised Israel would be to him "a kingdom of priests, and a holy nation." Both the Hebrew and Greek words for "holy" mean something or someone set apart for God's service. In the New Testament the noun may also be translated as "saint" or "sanctified one." The word "saint" was used when speaking of a Christian. Both of Paul's letters to the Corinthian church are addressed to the "saints" in Corinth. While they did not act very saintly, they were saints by virtue of their faith in Jesus Christ.

It is significant that the writer of Exodus said that Israel was to be a "kingdom of priests" (note the plural). This means that each person who kept the covenant was a priest whose responsibility was to bring pagan people to God. Peter carries this idea over into the Christian faith in the sense that *all* believers in Christ are priests (1 Pet. 2:5, 9), and from this comes the Christian concept of the priesthood of believers–everyone is chosen to be a priest. As we move ahead now into the rest of this book, we will examine the various aspects of this principle.

A Perversion of the Principle

The firm belief in the principle of the priesthood of believers was accepted completely in the apostolic church. However, as the years passed, the "competency of the soul in religion" was held in question. Over the centuries the Roman church developed an ecclesiastical system that centered power in the clergy, and Innocent I (A.D. 402—417) became the first bishop of Rome to claim universal jurisdiction over the church based on the tradition that Peter had been the first bishop of Rome.[4]

Historian Robert Baker[5] believes that this tradition came much later, and according to some outstanding Catholic writers Innocent's claim can never be proved. Dr. Baker takes the position that Leo I (440—461) "may rightly be called the first pope."[6] At any rate, with the passing of the centuries, a complex hierarchical system of church orders emerged in which deacons, pastors, and bishops–priests–assumed control. The autonomy of the local church disappeared and the principle of the priesthood of believers gave way to the priestly order and functions.[7] However, throughout this period various small groups struggled valiantly to hold to the traditional New Testament principle of the priesthood of all believers, but because of official opposition and persecution they were largely driven underground.

The Protestant Reformation

Timothy George labels the two centuries before the time of the Protestant Reformers "The Age of Anxiety." He goes on to say, "While abuses abounded in the church, so did cries for reform. New forms of lay piety, devotional treatises in the vernacular, renewed interest in relics, pilgrimages, saints, and popular religious movements–the Lollards in England, the Hussites in Bohemia, the Waldensians and Spiritual Franciscans in Italy and France–testified to a deep-seated and somewhat frenetic spirituality. Indeed, we see a steady growth in the power and depth of religious feelings right up to the time of the Reformation."[8]

While there were other great reformers–Huldreich Zwingli, John Calvin, and Menno Simons–the Protestant Reformation is synonymous with the name of Martin Luther. To quote historian Timothy George again, "The sixteenth century was an age of violence and coercion, and the mainline reformers were not completely innocent of bigotry and intolerance."[9] But they rendered undying service in recapturing and rescuing the basic truths of the New Testament. For our purpose here we will focus upon Martin Luther. In doing so I will rely heavily on the comments of Timothy George.

Dr. George calls his treatment of Luther, "Yearning for Grace." According to Dr. George, "Luther's greatest contribution to the Protestant ecclesiology was his doctrine of the priesthood of believers." (I would say that he rediscovered this doctrine, which had been in the New Testament from the beginning.) Then he defines Luther's position of the priesthood of believers in one sentence, "Every Christian is someone else's priest, and we are all priests to one another."[10]

It was Luther's belief that every Christian is a priest by virtue of his or her baptism.[11] The priesthood is derived from Christ. Quoting Luther directly, "We are priests as he is Priest, sons as he is Son, kings as he is King." Furthermore, Luther insisted that priestly prerogatives belong to all Christians, not to a select caste of holy men. And he based his view that all Christians are priests in equal degree on two New Testament verses, "Ye are . . . a royal priesthood" (1 Pet. 2:9) and "[Thou] hath made us kings and priests" (Rev. 1:6).

I have two problems with Luther's view at this point. If all Christians are priests, yet baptism is necessary for a person to be a priest, then his position implies belief in what we refer to as baptismal regeneration. Also his view that "every Christian is someone else's priest, and we are all priests to one another" ignores the idea that every Christian has free access to God. It is my view that this denies the principle of the competency of the soul in religion. In this respect Luther's thinking was still influenced by his Catholic theology.

Furthermore, Luther sought to regulate the preaching ministry of Christian "priests." It was his opinion that the ministry of the Word was the primary task of the church. Every Christian had the right to preach–an exercise that was to be expressed freely in the midst of non-Christians. But in a Christian community (the local church), this right should be conferred upon a person chosen for that role within that church; in turn, that person would be responsible to the congregation. Luther believed that "what we give to him today we can take away from him tomorrow." Note the strong statement for a congregational form of government. As for ordination, Luther believed the act did not confer special authority or grace. "It was merely the public means by which one is commissioned through prayer, Scripture, and the laying on of hands to serve the congregation."[12]

Luther excluded women, children, and persons without competence from exercising an official ministry in the church. However, he did agree that in times of emergency they could be allowed to fulfill that role by virtue of their participation in the priesthood of all believers.[13]

We may not agree with Martin Luther on all points, but there can be no question that he, through the powerful forces of the Reformation, rescued the vital doctrine of the priesthood of believers from oblivion. Yes, over the centuries there were smaller groups of Christians who attempted to follow the New Testament principle. But we can ever be grateful to Luther for his trumpet blast on behalf of "soul freedom."

The Continuing Struggle

While the efforts of Luther and his fellow reformers achieved a great deal, the struggle for individual priesthood was far from over. For one thing, the church at Rome did not make the Bible available to the people. It was not written in the language of the people, and it was believed only the ordained priests could interpret it.

Luther made the Bible available in German. The names of those in England who made the Bible available in their native tongue read like a "roll call of the faithful." In 1382 John Wycliffe published his English translation. William Tyndale issued his New Testament in 1525, and Miles Coverdale put out his translation in 1535.

In England there was a struggle over separation of church and state. Thomas Helwys, a Baptist layman, stands out in this struggle. Leon McBeth says Helwys "was ahead of his time in asking religious liberty for all people. In perhaps the most inclusive liberty statement of those years [*A Short Declaration of the Mystery of Iniquity, 1612*, addressed personally to King James], Helwys said, 'Let them be heretikes, Turcks, Jewes, or whatsoever it apperteynes not to the earthly power to punish them in the least measure' in religious matters. Helwys's reasoned defense of liberty for such groups as Roman Catholics, Jews, and Moslems probably cost him some support he might have enjoyed otherwise."[14]

Despite the efforts of Helwys and others, religious persecution continued. The early American colonists fled England to escape religious persecution. Tragically, though, as soon as they got settled, they organized established churches and persecuted any and all dissenters. This was especially true in Massachusetts and Virginia. However, some colonists, such as Baptist preacher John Leland, resisted. Leland became the shining star in the struggle for religious liberty in colonial America.

In the 1930s a Methodist layman, Frank Mead, wrote a book entitled *See These Banners Go* in which he discussed a number of church denominations. In speaking of the persecution endured by Baptists for absolute religious liberty, Mead said, "Never once in their bitter, bloody history have they struck back at their persecutors or persecuted any other for his faith. That is patriotism touched by the divine."[15]

Throughout all this, Baptists and others joined in insistence upon the priesthood of all believers. This principle was preserved at a great price. In a real sense it should be preserved and practiced today.

3. The Priesthood of the Believer: Privilege and Responsibility

According to tradition, one of Alexander the Great's soldiers was brought before him accused of cowardice in battle. When the great conqueror asked him his name, he replied, "Alexander, sire." To that Alexander responded, "Either change your ways or else change your name."

No doubt, to a military man it was considered a privilege to be one of Alexander's soldiers. But with the privilege there was also a greater responsibility. Jesus endorsed this rule of life when he said, "For unto whomsoever much is given, of him shall be much required: and to whom men have committed much, of him they will ask the more" (Luke 12:48).

Privilege and responsibility go hand in hand. If this is true at the human level, it is much more so at the divine-human level. Unfortunately, though, most people are willing to accept privilege, but few are willing to accept the attendant responsibilities.

But as a friend of mine said, "Grace is free but it makes its demands."It was at this point that the people of Israel failed in their covenant relationship with the Lord. They were perfectly willing to be his "peculiar treasure" and even to be a "kingdom of priests," but they were not willing to assume the accompanying responsibilities.

Jesus urged his would-be followers, then and now, to count the cost of following him (Matt. 9:19—20; Luke 14:26—31). And in counting that cost it is important that we consider carefully both the privileges and responsibilities involved in the principle of the priesthood of the believer.

Privileges of Our Priesthood.

Certain privileges are inherent in the principle of the priesthood of the believer. Without question, to be a believer means that we have had a personal saving experience with God in Christ. And this experience gives us direct access to God.

A Christian leader of a past generation wrote, "All men have an equal right to direct access to God."[1] Hardly anyone will question our right of access to God. But the key word in this axiom is "direct." And direct access to God means that nothing stands between us and God–not government, church, saint, priest, or law.

This truth is graphically illustrated by a phenomenon that occurred immediately after Jesus' death on the cross: "And behold the veil of the temple was rent in twain from the top to the bottom; and the earth did quake, and the rocks rent" (Matt. 27:51). (We're told in the Jewish Talmud that a quake rocked the Temple forty years before its destruction in A.D. 70. This would be A.D 30, the year when Jesus died.) But the veil referred to here is the heavy one that separated the Holy of Holies from the Holy Place. The people had no access to these sacred rooms; only the priests could enter the Holy Place, and only the high priest could pass through the veil into the Holy of Holies–and then just once a year on the Day of Atonement.

The fact that the veil was torn from top to bottom shows that it was an act of God, and now through Christ's death everyone had direct access to God through faith in his Son. In a sense God had opened up all the courts of the Temple so that all people might through faith in Christ come directly to the Father. This marvelous truth will be discussed in greater detail in chapter 4.

Growing out of this free access to God through faith are additional privileges for the Christian believer. One of these is the privilege of praying directly to God. It is true that other believers can pray for us, but no one else can pray in our stead. In other words, we do not need a priest or a saint to pray for us in order for God to hear our requests.

Further, we're instructed to pray in Jesus' name (John 16:23). This does not mean a rote calling or repeating of his name. Neither is it a blank check or a "name it and claim it" promise. Rather, "name" refers to the total person of Jesus Christ–his complete and redeeming work as our high priest who knows our weaknesses and yet has made us priests who can "come boldly unto the throne of grace, that we may obtain mercy, and find grace to help in time of need" (Heb. 4:16).

In writing to the Christians at Philippi, the apostle Paul says nothing about the need for a human intermediary when he writes, "Be careful [overly anxious] for nothing; but in every thing by prayer and supplication with thanksgiving let your requests be made known unto God" (Phil. 4:6).

Someone said that God has had only one Son who lived without sin, but he has never had a son who lived without prayer. And the greatest pray-er the world has ever known lived the greatest life the world has ever seen. In every great crisis in Jesus' life he was sustained by prayer: at his baptism (Luke 3:21), before choosing the twelve apostles (Luke 6:12—13), at his transfiguration (Luke 9:29), in Gethsemane (Luke 22:41—44), and at Calvary (Luke 23:34).

If Jesus needed to pray, how much more we need to pray! And as we follow his example, we know that through him we have full access to the Father.

Another privilege that is really a part of prayer is the confession of our sins directly to God. There is no evidence in the Bible that we should confess them to a priest or to anyone else with a view to receiving God's forgiveness. But we do have the glorious promise that "if we confess our sins, he [God] is faithful and just to forgive us our sins, and to cleanse us from all unrighteousness" (1 John 1:9).

Then again, the writer of James says, "Confess your faults [sins] one to another, and pray for one another, that ye may be healed" (James 5:16). And Dr. A. T. Robertson, noted Bible scholar, wrote "Confession of sin to God is already assumed. But public confession of certain sins to one another in the meetings is greatly helpful in many ways. This is not confessing to one man like a priest in place of the public confession. One may confess to the pastor without confessing to God or to the church, with little benefit to anybody."[2]

Pope Leo I based his authority, and through him that of the priesthood, to forgive or to retain sins on Matt. 16:19: "And I will give unto thee the keys of the kingdom of heaven: and whatsoever thou shalt bind on earth shall be bound in heaven: and whatsoever thou shalt loose on earth shall be loosed in heaven." This reads as if actions taken on earth will later be affirmed in heaven. If this is the meaning, then Jesus gave the same authority to every local church (Matt. 18:18).

Unfortunately, however, this is not a good translation of the Greek text. Literally, it reads, "Shall have been bound . . . shall have been loosed in heaven." Some interpreters see the "keys" as a symbol of rabbinical authority. But taken in the natural sense, "keys" lock and unlock doors. Consequently, I interpret "keys" as referring to the gospel, which opens the door to the kingdom of heaven.

Jesus committed the gospel to believers everywhere. If we bind it on earth by not witnessing to it, "heaven" has already declared that there is no other way it can be preached to a lost world. On the other hand, if we loose the gospel on earth by proclaiming it, "heaven" has already declared that many will hear, some will believe, and those who believe will be saved. As believers, we are the stewards of the gospel. It is a great privilege. But it is a greater responsibility!

Still another privilege involved in the teaching on the priesthood of the believer is the right to read and interpret the Scriptures as we are led by the Holy Spirit, and not according to our particular bias. On the surface it would appear that the wording of 2 Pet. 1:20 refutes this idea, "Knowing this first, that no prophecy of the scripture is of any private interpretation."

However, it is interesting to read certain other modern translations. For example, "You must understand this in the first place, that no prophecy in Scripture can be understood through one's own powers" (Goodspeed). The Moffatt translation stresses the importance of our understanding "that no prophetic scripture allows a man to interpret it by himself." Charles Williams words it this way: "no prophecy in Scripture is to be interpreted by one's own mind." Robertson reads "no prophecy of Scripture comes out of private disclosure."[3] And J. B. Phillips best expresses the thought of the Greek wording, "But you must understand this at the outset, that no prophecy of scripture *arose from an individual's interpretation of the truth*" (italics mine). Each translation emphasizes our need of the Holy Spirit's aid in understanding the Scriptures, which is in complete harmony with the principle of the priesthood of the believer.

A literal translation of 2 Pet. 1:20 reads, "Knowing this first, that no single part of the whole prophetic writing comes into being by one's own disclosure." In other words, the human mind is incapable of itself of interpreting God's Word. Dr. Robertson builds on this idea in saying that "no prophet starts a prophecy himself. He is not a self-starter."[4]

The writer of 2 Peter then adds, "For the prophecy came not in old time by the will of man: but holy men of God spake as they were *moved by the Holy Ghost*" (2 Pet. 1:21, italics mine). The original Greek word translated "were moved" literally means "to bear." The idea here is that those men who spoke or wrote the Scriptures were "borne along by the Holy Spirit," that is, they spoke "from God."

This same idea is supported by the apostle Paul in his letter to young Timothy in which he says, "Every single part of the whole of Scripture is God-breathed" (2 Tim. 3:16, my literal translation of the original Greek). This simply means the same God who through his Spirit breathed his Word into the hearts and minds of the writers of Scripture, gives us–believers–the privilege of interpreting them under the leadership of his Holy Spirit.

Responsibilities of the Believer

As priests of God each of us bears responsibilities commensurate with the privileges involved. These responsibilities are related to who you are and what you do.

As priests of God, we must be holy. The Lord made this clear to Moses: "Speak unto all the congregation of the children of Israel, and say unto them, Ye shall be holy: for I the Lord your God am holy" (Lev. 19:2).

As mentioned earlier, the Hebrew and Greek words for "holy" imply separation. For instance, anyone or anything set apart for the service of God or a god was called holy. In pagan religions that had sex deities, women were used by men in the sex act as worship of a given deity. They were for that reason called "holy" women. For example, the principal deity of Corinth was Aphrodite, the goddess of sex. Her temple was located on the Acrocorinthus, eighteen hundred feet above the city. At one time there were one thousand of these holy women, or temple prostitutes, in Corinth.

The word "holy" did not have a moral content until it came to be used of the Lord God (Isa. 6:1—3). This simply means now that as a priest of the Lord each of us must live in keeping with *God's* holy, righteous nature. If we are to serve Christ, we must be Christlike, and we *are* holy because we have been set apart for God's service. And to be effective in that role, we must be Godlike. The basic asset in Christian service is character. No matter how gifted we are, if our character is suspect, our talents carry little weight or meaning.

I believe Paul had this in mind when he wrote to the Christians in Ephesus, "I therefore, the prisoner of the Lord, beseech you that ye walk worthy of the vocation wherewith ye are called" (Eph. 4:1). The word "walk" refers to our manner of life. But the key word in this verse is "worthy," and it is derived from a Greek word that is descriptive of scales or balances. And the picture we have in this verse is of a balance—two pans suspended from a crossbar. If a customer ordered five pounds of sugar, the merchant placed a five-pound weight in one of the pans. Then he put a container in the other pan and poured sugar into it until the weight of the sugar balanced the five-pound weight.

So what Paul is actually saying here is that we are to place our calling or vocation in one pan and our manner of life in the other pan. The strength, or weight, or our lifestyle should be in perfect balance with our calling as Christians. The translators of the New English Bible worded it this way, "As God has called you, live up to your calling."

Further, as Christian priests, our lives are to be characterized by love. The writer of 1 John said that "God is love" (4:8), and he could no more stop loving than he could stop being God. The word used for love in this verse is *agapē*.

The Greek language had three principal words for love. *Eros* referred to erotic love and is not found in the New Testament. The word *philia* referred to the warm love of friendship. And the third word is *agapē*. The Greeks regarded it as a cold word, so it was used sparingly in the classical writings. But *agapē* love is a powerful New Testament word. It seems that the Holy Spirit chose this word to express the highest kind of love, the love that characterizes the very nature of God. Someone suggested that it means absolute loyalty to its object. My New Testament professor in seminary said that the one English word that most nearly translates *agapē* is "selflessness."

It was this love that moved God to give his only begotten Son as our redeemer (John 3:16). It was this love that led Jesus to the cross on our behalf (John 13:1). And it was this love that Jesus said Christians should have for one another (John 15:12). It is God's love coming down to us, our love through faith in Christ rising to him, and it is our love going out to other people–the final test of *agapē* love.

Of course, it is difficult to love some people. But even if we do not like a person or agree with that person's lifestyle, we can *agapē* love him or her. Paul gave us the pattern when he wrote,

"God commendeth his love toward us, in that, while we were yet sinners [God's enemies], Christ died for us" (Rom. 5:8). If God loved us that way, surely as his priests we must love as he does. One of my seminary professors used to say that we will love one another in heaven, so we should start practicing it on earth.

Perhaps the most powerful essay every written on love is found in our Bible (1 Cor. 13) and it is often referred to as the "love chapter." It has even been called Paul's "Ode to Love." In fact, though, it is the climax of a carefully reasoned argument in which Paul was dealing with controversy in the church at Corinth (1 Corinthians 12—14). It is Paul's superhighway out of a jungle of controversy into the beautiful valley of peace (1 Cor. 12:31b).

In recent years we have seen many of our denominations embroiled in strife over such things as ecclesiology and theology. Unfortunately, such wranglings give a negative witness to Christ and his love. But we never learn because this sort of thing has been going on since Jesus established his new society. In fact, it was a dispute among Jesus' disciples that precipitated his command that they love one another.

A thorough interpretation of 1 Corinthians 13 would require a book of great proportions, but it can be outlined briefly: (1) The Necessity of Love (13:1—3); (2) The Nature of Love (13:4—7); (3) The Abiding Quality of Love (13:8—13). I will now expand that outline by emphasizing three crucial truths.

First, no matter how talented we are and how zealous we are to use those talents for the Lord, if we do so out of any motivation other than love, Paul says we are "nothing," a zero (13:2—3). People can sense whether or not we love them, and when everything else fails, they will respond to love.

Almost fifty years ago my friend Dr. L. R. Scarborough, a former seminary president and great evangelist, told me this story. One summer he preached in a revival in a rural church near Mineral Wells, Texas. In the community was an unsaved man who through the years had resisted the efforts of many preachers to lead him to Christ.

Dr. Scarborough was not successful either. But several months later, Dr. Scarborough's phone rang at 11:00 P.M., getting him out of bed. It was this man calling; after identifying himself, he said, "I am under conviction and want you to come and tell me how to be saved." Though it was a bitterly cold night and the roads were covered with snow and ice, Dr. Scarborough said, "I'll be there as soon as I can get there."

After a drive of over fifty miles, he arrived at the man's house about 2:30 in the morning. Within just ten minutes, the man had accepted Jesus as his Savior. Afterwards he said, "I suppose you wonder why I would ask you to get out on a night like this. Well, last summer you said that God loved my soul and you loved my soul. I wanted to know if you meant it. If you came out on a night like this, I knew that you did. Had you said you would come tomorrow or when the weather moderated, you might just as well not have come."As one of God's priests, my friend had shown that he shared God's love for that man.

Second, Paul wrote that, "Love suffers long, and is kind" (1 Cor. 13:4). "Suffers long" or "long-suffering" means that Christian love suffers the evil done to it for a long time before striking back. Love has a long fuse on its temper. The words, "is kind," go a step father. They mean that love attempts in every way possible to reward evil with good.

Third, Paul writes that love "thinketh no evil" (1 Cor. 13:5). Love does not keep books on evil done to it with a view to evening the score. As God's priests, we need this kind of love!

The priesthood of the believer also involves what we do. Christianity is not a spectator faith. We must come out of the stands into the arena and get involved.

Earlier I expressed my strong feelings against Christians being separated into clergy and laity. The word "clergy" is not in the Bible. The word "laity" comes from the Greek word *laos*, meaning people. All believers in Christ are the people of God, and as such, we are all to be busy for God.

Whatever Saul of Tarsus (Paul) did, he with all his might. When he was persecuting Christians, he did it with vengeance—like a war-horse, breathing and snorting as though eager for battle (Acts 9:1). But following his Damascus road experience, his first question was "What shall I do, Lord?" (Acts 22:10). Years later he could in all truth say to Agrippa, "I was not disobedient unto the heavenly vision" (Acts 26:19). He was constantly busy for his Lord.

As believers we have the privilege of reading and interpreting the Scriptures for ourselves under the leadership of the Holy Spirit. But we also have the responsibility of studying the Scriptures in order properly to interpret them.

Paul describes most of us when he calls his readers "babes in Christ" (1 Cor. 3:1)–babes who were still on a milk diet (3:2). The writer of Hebrews expressed it this way, "For when for the time ye ought to be teachers, ye have need that one teach you again which be the first principles [ABC's] of the oracles of God; and are become such as have need of milk, and not of strong meat. For every one that useth milk is unskillful in the word of righteousness: for he is a babe. But strong meat belongeth to them that are of full age [mature Christians], even those who by reason of use have their senses exercised to discern both good and evil" (Heb. 5:12—14).

Most interpreters of Hebrews see these words as a warning to Hebrew Christians not to forsake Christ to return to Judaism, thus losing their salvation. I see them, though, as a warning against people's refusal to develop and fulfill their place in God's redemptive mission and purpose–for redeeming all people who receive Christ as Savior.[5]

The writer of Hebrews bases his warning on Israel's rebellion at Kadesh-barnea, their refusal to enter Canaan, the land of their destiny (Numbers 14). The theme is not that of lost salvation, but of lost opportunity. The keynote of Hebrews is not "Do not go back," but "Let us go on unto perfection," or to the fulfillment of our role in God's redemptive purpose (Heb. 6:1).[6] Tragically, many Christians lose their opportunity to be used effectively for God because they are not adequately prepared.

We need more "Berean Christians." When Paul went to Berea and preached in the synagogue about Jesus beIng the fulfillment of the Jewish messianic prophecies, the people "received the word with all readiness of mind, and searched the scriptures daily, whether these things were so" (Acts 17:11). Their minds were open to new truth, but they knew their Scriptures and knew what Paul taught was true.

So many Christians when asked what they believe will reply, "I believe what my denomination [Baptist, Episcopal, Lutheran, Methodist, Presbyterian, etc.] believes." When asked what their denomination believes, they will reply, "I don't know. But I believe it!"

There is no excuse for this. While most church groups have literature explaining their beliefs, the Bible is to be our sourcebook. It is true, of course, that not all believer-priests have a working knowledge of the original languages of the Bible, Hebrew and Greek. But everyone has access to commentaries and other Bible study helps. One of the most helpful tools in my library is a three-volume set of *Twenty-Six Translations of the Bible*. Its basic text is the King James Version, but each verse is illuminated by wording from significant modern language versions.

Then there are those who excuse themselves because "we just can't understand it." Of course they can't! If they tried to read and understand a simple novel the way they read the Bible–skipping and hopping around, reading a sentence here and a paragraph there–they would never understand the story. But if we read God's Word with hungry and open hearts, vistas of truth will open before our eyes. Jesus promises that the same Holy Spirit who inspired the Scripture writers "will guide you into all [spiritual] truth" (John 16:13).

The Bible, even the English versions, contains truth yet to be comprehended. We may be able to learn all there is to know about human-made books, but this is not true of the Bible because it is the revelation of God's infinite wisdom. I am in debt to my two New Testament seminary professors for the following ideas.

Professor W. Hersey Davis once told our class that most preachers harrow over their favorite passages in preaching. To anyone not familiar with agricultural terms, "harrow" means merely to scratch the surface. Consequently, when most preachers announce a text, the listeners usually have a pretty good idea what's going to be said. Professor Davis then said, "Set your plow to go down deep and turn up some rich, fertile soil." This way we can catch the richness of God's word.

Professor A. T. Robertson was perhaps the greatest New Testament scholar of his generation. I was in his senior Greek class the day he had a stroke; he died an hour and a half later. This happened on Monday, September 24, 1934, but just the Friday before he gave us what was perhaps his greatest testimony concerning the Scriptures. He said, "For more than fifty years I have studied the New Testament. But I never open my Greek New Testament without finding something I never saw before." The same can be said for most of us as we study our English Bible if we are open and sensitive to the teaching of the Holy Spirit.

One final word of advice. In interpreting the Scriptures each of us is responsible for our interpretation. But the standard by which the Bible is to be interpreted is Jesus Christ. He is God's full revelation of himself. Consequently, any interpretation that is contrary to him and his teaching is wrong.

Finally, the priesthood of the believer involves the responsibility of ministering to fellow believers and of sharing the gospel with nonbelievers. The Lord's covenant called Israel to be a nation of priests who were constantly attempting to win pagan people to worship and serve the true God. In Peter's description of the Christian's priesthood he said they are to "shew forth the praises of him who hath called you out of darkness into his excellent light" (1 Pet. 2:9). The meaning is sharper in a more recent translation in which as believer-priests we are "entrusted with the proclamation of the goodness" of God's redemption in Christ (Twentieth Century New testament).

It is a great privilege to be a priest of our Lord. But it is an even greater responsibility.

4. The Priesthood of the Believer and Salvation

The term "priesthood of the believer" implies salvation. In fact, salvation is where the principle of the priesthood of the believer begins. In discussing the history of this teaching, we began with God's covenant with Israel at Mt. Sinai.

God had just redeemed Israel from the bondage of Egypt (Exod. 20:2). Then he proposed to make Israel a nation of priests. Because of this we believe that every person who has been saved from sin through faith in Jesus Christ is to be a Christian *priest* (1 Pet. 2:9–10).

In speaking of salvation it is necessary to explore the answers to certain questions. Is salvation available to everyone? Is it possible to be saved by law? Why must salvation be by grace through faith? What is God's part in salvation? What is our part in salvation?

God's Sovereignty and Our Free Will

There is no question that the Bible teaches the sovereignty of God. At the same time the Bible clearly teaches that we are persons of free will. On the surface, it would appear that these doctrines are in conflict. If so, the Bible contradicts itself, a proposition that most Christians deny.

As we confront this problem, it will be helpful to define these doctrines in simple terms. God's sovereignty means God can act as he wills, in keeping with his benevolent, righteous nature and purpose, without the advice or consent of anyone outside himself.

On the other hand, we as people can exercise our free will because we were created in God's image as spiritual persons and are endowed with the privilege of choice, and in that freedom we are capable of dealing with God directly. In fact, we are God's only creatures who can say "no" to him. It is important to remember, though, that in the Bible God never arbitrarily coerces people against their will.

God's sovereignty is not that of a cruel tyrant who is unmindful of the welfare of his subjects. He is a loving, merciful, redeeming God who wills to do the greatest amount of good for the greatest number of his people. At the same time, he is not a permissive God who ignores people's sins. And he can forgive sin only upon a condition that is in keeping with his holy, righteous nature. However, God will not force us to accept those conditions contrary to the exercise of our own free wills. To do so would reduce us from people to puppets, and he loves us too much to destroy our personhood. If we were not free to make choices, God would be responsible for our sins, and that is unthinkable.

Many interpreters believe that these two self-evident truths—God's sovereignty and human free will—cannot be harmonized. But I believe they can be harmonized when properly understood. Ignoring certain proof texts, which are subject to interpretation, I want to focus our attention on what Paul has to say in Ephesians concerning what has come to be known theologically as the doctrine of election. Paul writes that God has elected or "chosen" (Eph. 1:4) a plan of salvation (Eph. 1–2) and a people to propagate that plan (Eph. 3–6). People are free to accept or reject either or both. This idea agrees with both the soul's competency in religion and the priesthood of the believer. Note that God did this "before the foundation of the world" (Eph. 1:4). The writer of Revelation speaks of Christ as "the Lamb slain from the foundation of the world" (13:8). So forgiveness was in the heart of God before sin was in the heart of people.

Referring again to Eph. 1:4, the last two words, "in love," really belong in verse 5, which would then read, "In love having predestinated us unto the adoption of children by [through] Jesus Christ to himself, according to the good pleasure of his will." Here Paul uses the Roman legal term "adoption," which means "placing as a son." Under the Roman law an adopted son was said to be born again into a new family. Jesus expressed the same idea when he speaks of the necessity of being "born again" (John 3:3).

The words "having predestinated" are the key phrase in Eph. 1:5. Unfortunately, many interpret the meaning from the English word rather than from the Greek word, *proorisas*. The basic verb is *horizō* from which comes our word "horizon." When we stand and look out to where the earth and sky seem to meet, that is the horizon, or the limit or boundary of our vision from where we stand. *Horizō* means "to set a boundary." So, with the prefix *pro*, predestinated, means to set a boundary beforehand or before creation. The boundary is expressed by the phrase "in Christ."

So God set a boundary beforehand. Then in his sovereignty, God, without the advice or consent of anyone outside himself, said that all in Christ—will be saved, and everyone outside Christ will be lost. It is interesting to notice that in Eph. 1:3–10 the phrase "in Christ" or its equivalent appears ten times.

But having set the boundary, God left people free to choose whether to be in Christ or outside of him. This defines our free will, and it is seen in the words, "after that ye believed" (Eph. 1:13b). Now we see that God set the condition of salvation (sovereignty), and he left people free to accept or reject the plan (free will). Consequently, the two are in complete harmony. And this agrees with humanity's soul competency out of which comes the principle of the priesthood of the believer.

In Ephesians 2 Paul goes on to show how this plan of salvation works. In the first century, the Jews divided the human race into Jews and Gentiles. They believed that Gentiles were outside the circle of God's love. But Paul shows how in Christ

God has made both Jews and Gentiles one and has given both direct access to him. Outside of Christ both are lost from God and must be saved by grace through faith (Eph. 2:1–10).

But in his death and resurrection, Christ has "broken down the middle wall of partition between us" (Eph. 2:14). In the Jerusalem Temple, at each entrance from the Court of the Gentiles into the Court of the Women, large limestone slabs were fastened to the wall. On each was a written warning prohibiting Gentiles from going beyond that point. To do so incurred the penalty of death. This meant that no Gentile had any access whatever to God.

In Christ's atoning death those signs were removed. His purpose was "to make in himself of twain one new man, so making peace" (Eph. 2:15). No longer was there the distinction between Jew and Gentile. In Christ God established a whole new order—Christians. Now, one Jew plus one Gentle plus Christ equals two Christians. Any combination of racial distinctions placed in this equation gives the same answer, as both Jews and Gentiles are reconciled "unto God in one body by the cross, having slain the enmity thereby" (Eph. 2:18). Removing the wall of partition, like this torn veil (p. 25), gives further direct access to God. Remember, the people in Ephesus who received this letter from Paul were both Jews and Gentiles who had become Christians.

In the remaining chapters of Ephesians, Paul directs his attention to people elected or chosen to propagate God's plan of salvation. But as with the plan so with the people—each redeemed person was free to accept or reject the role. Once again we see both God's sovereignty and our free will in operation.

As the apostle to the Gentiles Paul had accepted his role of the priesthood of the believer—to declare the "mystery of Christ" (Eph. 3:1–3). In the Christian sense, a mystery was something that could not be known through human reason; it must be received through divine revelation. And what is that mystery? Paul explains, "That the Gentiles should be fellow-heirs, and of the same body, and partakers of his promise in Christ by the gospel" (Eph. 3:6). This sounds "old hat" today, but in the first century it was social and religious dynamite.

The body Paul refers to in that verse is "the church, which is his body, the fullness of him that filleth all in all" (Eph. 1:22–23). Here Paul uses the word "church" in the general sense of all the people of God. But since he was writing to a group of churches in the Roman province of Asia, the role applies to each local church, even to every believer in each one. Our role as priests of God is so that there "might be known by [through] the church the manifold wisdom of God, according to the eternal purpose which he purposed in Christ Jesus our Lord" (Eph. 3:10–11).

We've seem in this brief overview of Ephesians the marvelous harmony between God's sovereignty and our free will. God in his sovereignty set forth both the *plan* and the *people* to propagate it, and we are free to accept either or both. However, we need God far more than he needs us, and if we reject either or both, we are the losers. God's redemptive purpose will proceed. But in our rejection we are left behind. God has often changed his people but never his purpose. Each segment of the Christian faith should be attentive to this warning.

Law and Grace

Not let us examine another question concerning the priesthood of the believer and salvation. This has to do with law and grace.

Is it possible for a person to be saved by keeping the Ten Commandments? The answer is "yes." Jesus himself said so (Mark 10:17, 19). When the rich young ruler asked, "Good Master, what shall I do that I may inherit eternal life?" Jesus replied by quoting the last six of the Ten Commandments having to do with our relation to other people. Note the omission of the first four dealing with our relation to God. Jesus did this with design.

Though the man had a good relationship with other people, he had not kept the last six commandments perfectly. This became evident as the conversation proceeded.

The first four commandments are involved in Jesus' demand that he sell all his goods and give the proceeds to feed the poor (Mark 10:21a). Jesus does not demand that every believer take the poverty oath. In this case the man's wealth was his god. He was unwilling to forsake this and follow the rugged road that Jesus proposed.

Furthermore, the man's refusal also showed that he had not fully obeyed the last six commandments. So he went away grieved (Mark 10:22).

The hitch in this matter is that to be saved by keeping the Ten Commandments, you must keep every one of them perfectly. Possible? Yes. But totally improbable! The writer of James made this clear when he said, "For whosoever shall keep the whole law, and yet offend in one point, he is guilty of all" (2:10).

Now this introduces another question. If a person living in a pagan land never sees a Bible, never hears the name of Jesus, and never hears a gospel sermon—is he lost from God? Again the answer is "yes." In writing to the Christians in Rome, Paul speaks of the Jews as having God's law written on parchment but states that the pagan has God's law written in his heart: "For as many as have sinned without law shall also perish without law: and as many as have sinned in the law shall be judged by the law. . . . [F]or when the Gentiles, which have not the law, do by nature the things contained in the law, these having not the law, are a law unto themselves: Which shew the work of the law written in their hearts, their conscience also bearing witness, and their thoughts the meanwhile accusing or else excusing one another; in the day when God shall judge the secrets of men by Jesus Christ according to my gospel" (Rom. 2:12, 14–16).

This raises another question. If a person does as good as he or she knows, will that person be saved? Once more the answer is "yes." But no one does as good as he or she knows to do.

God's final judgment will be based upon the degree of knowledge of God's will against which a person has sinned. Jesus taught degrees of punishment in hell. Luke quotes Jesus as saying, "And that servant, which knew his lord's will, and prepared not himself, neither did according to his will, shall be beaten with many stripes. But he that knew not, and did commit things worthy of stripes, shall be beaten with few stripes. For unto whomsoever much is given, of him shall be much required" (Luke 12:47–48).

As priests of God we may be concerned about the pagans in some foreign land but have little concern about our unsaved neighbor who has a Bible (whether or not he reads it)and is familiar with God's revelation in Christ. Both demand our attention!

The story is told of a young man who came to evangelist Charles Haddon Spurgeon with a question, "Will the heathen be saved if we do not preach the gospel to him?" Mr. Spurgeon replied, "Are we saved if we do not preach the gospel to him?" Or to our neighbor for that matter. It is a question to ponder.

Still another question arises. Is God fair in his demand regarding his law? Again, we have to say "yes." Having concluded that "all have sinned, and come short of the glory of God" (Rom. 3:23), Paul proceeds to show what God in Christ has done to offer a way of escape from this predicament. In Christ God has declared "his righteousness: that he might be just, and the justifier of him which believeth in Jesus" (Rom. 3:26).

Someone said that for Jesus to live in a flesh and blood body, to be tempted in all things like as we are, and not sin one time, is as great a miracle in the moral sphere as the virgin birth is in the biological sphere. But in doing so, Jesus proved that God was just in his demand. Then having done this, as the sinless one, he submitted to the cross that he might become the *justifier* of all who believe in Jesus. For "God was in Christ, reconciling the world unto himself" (2 Cor. 5:19).

Suppose some lost person comes to the final judgment and says, "God, I did my best to keep your law. But I could not do it. No one can do it. And you are unjust in demanding it!" The Father will point to the Son and say, "One did. If one could, everyone could!" It is not that a person cannot keep God's law; it is that he or she wills not to do so.

And this is exactly why salvation must be by grace through faith, apart from law! When people by law failed to ascend the heights to God, in the person of his Son God came down to us to provide a way for us to be with him. The writer of the Gospel of John spells this out clearly when he quoted Jesus, "I am the way, the truth, and the life: no one cometh unto the Father but by [through] me" (John 14:6).

Basically, the Greek verb for "grace" meant to make a gift, then to forgive a debt, to forgive a wrong, and, finally, to forgive sin. An old friend of mine once said that grace means that God gives us what we need, not what we deserve.

Jesus said that he came "to give his life a ransom for many" (Mark 10:45). "For many" is a Hebrew figure for "all." God paid the ransom to himself, that in the death of his Son he might provide the condition whereby a holy and righteous God could forgive our sins.

Perhaps the greatest single passage on salvation by grace through faith came to us through Paul when he wrote to the Christians in Ephesus, "For by grace you are being saved through faith, and that not out of yourselves, it is a gift of God: not out of works, lest anyone should boast. For we are his workmanship, created in Christ Jesus unto good works, which God before ordained in order that in them we should walk" (Eph. 2:8–10, my translation).

God's initiative is his sovereign grace. Our response is personal faith—the channel through which his grace flows into us. The source is neither ourselves nor our good works. This simply means that we have no grounds on which to boast. God is not in our debt, but we are in his, since it is all God's gift—even our ability to believe in Jesus. We are the product of God's creation through Christ Jesus. And though we are not created *by* our good works, we are created *for* good work.

These verses in Ephesians are the heart of the gospel that Paul preached to Jews and Gentiles alike. But when Paul and Barnabas began to preach this Good News to Gentiles, a group in the Jerusalem church called Judaizers objected strenuously (Acts 15:1–5). They believed that salvation was for Jews only and that in order for Gentiles to be saved they must first become Jewish proselytes, be circumcised, and live by the laws of Moses. This, however, would have been salvation by works *plus* faith, not by grace *through* faith. This created a major controversy in the church.

At the Jerusalem Conference in A.D. 49 (Acts 15; Galatians 2), Peter (out of his experience in the home of Cornelius, a Gentile [Acts 10]) says, "Why tempt ye God, to put a yoke upon the neck of the disciples, which neither our fathers nor we were able to bear? But we believe that by the grace of the Lord Jesus Christ we [Jews] shall be saved, even as they [Gentiles]" (Acts 15:10–11). The point was already made: instead of Gentiles becoming Jews before being saved, Peter said Jews must be saved the same way Gentiles are saved—by grace through faith in Jesus Christ. Fortunately, the early church leaders endorsed Paul's message, but the Judaizers continued to be a thorn in his side.

Over the centuries many things have been added to the simple plan of salvation given us by Paul: church membership, the ordinances, good works, and others. But none of these change the simple provision of Paul's word to the Ephesian Christians.

Take baptism for example. At the conclusion of Peter's magnificent sermon on the Day of Pentecost he said, "Repent, and be baptized every one of you in the name of Jesus Christ for the remission of sins" (Acts 2:38). The key word in this sentence is "for." The Greek preposition used here may be translated for, into, unto, as the result of, on the basis of, with respect to. The same preposition is used by Jesus in speaking of the people of Ninevah when he said, "They repented *at* the preaching of Jonas" (Matt. 12:41, italics mine). In other words, they repented as the result of his preaching.

We use the word "for" in the same sense. We say a man is executed *for* murder. We don't mean that he is executed in order to commit murder, but as the result of his having murdered. In the same wy, baptism is not in order for a person's sins to be remitted, but as the result of that person's sins having been remitted.

A similar idea is expressed by Peter when he speaks of Noah and the others in the ark as being "saved by water" (1 Pet. 3:20b). It isn't *by* water but *through* water. Then he goes on to say, "The like figure [antitype] whereunto even baptism doth also now save us" (1 Pet. 3:21a). All of this is to say that the eight people in the ark were not saved by being in the water. Instead, they were saved *through* the flood by being in the ark—the antitype of Christ.

The Greek language has two words for baptism, only one of which, *baptisma*, is used in the New Testament for Christian baptism. It denotes the meaning in the act, namely, what Jesus did for our salvation: he died, was buried, and rose again. Also it symbolizes what Jesus does in us as believers: we die to the old life, it is buried, and we rise to walk in a new life in Christ. This is the word used here and always for Christian baptism.

It is interesting that this word is not found in any Greek writings other than in the New Testament and subsequent ecclesiastical writings, which got it from the New Testament. It seems that the Holy Spirit coined this word to express the meaning in Christian baptism.

I have cited these two examples concerning baptism to illustrate the mistake of adding anything to salvation by grace through faith. The good works we do are the *fruit,* not the *root* of our salvation. Furthermore, anything a person does to or for the believer is not a requirement for salvation. It is a gift of God's work alone in and through Christ.

This agrees with the competency of the soul to have direct access to God and to deal with him alone. Furthermore, it enhances the priesthood of the believer who is responsible only to God.

Paul stresses this fact in writing to Timothy when he says, "For one God, and one mediator of God and of man, a man Christ Jesus, the one giving himself a ransom for all" (1 Tim. 2:5-6, my translation). A mediator was appointed by a judge to settle a difference between two people. He was to properly represent both and do everything necessary to bring them together in reconciliation. Christ Jesus was the God-Man; he had the nature of both God and human beings. He did everything necessary to bring them together. Consequently, it is in Christ Jesus that God and people meet in reconciliation. Christ is our only mediator. We need no other.

Threefold Nature of Salvation

Having come this far, we are now ready to consider the very heart of the principle of the priesthood of the believer and salvation, which is threefold in nature.

First, salvation is *regeneration*, new birth or birth from above. This is what Jesus refers to when he tells Nicodemus, "Except a man be born again [from above], he cannot see the kingdom of God" (John 3:3). Jesus is drawing an important comparison here in his conversation with Nicodemus (John 3:3-7). In natural birth a person is born into natural relationships, privileges, and responsibilities. But in the birth from above through the power of the Holy Spirit, we are born into spiritual relationships, privileges, and responsibilities, or into the kingdom of God.

In John 3:7 Jesus is saying, literally, "It is morally and spiritually necessary for you to be born again" or "from above."

Second, salvation is *sanctification*. Sanctification is the saving of the Christian life. The writer of Hebrews asks, "How shall we escape, if we neglect so great salvation?" Since he is writing to Hebrew Christians, the salvation referred to can hardly be regeneration. Instead the reference is to sanctification and the responsibilities related to that part of salvation.

Now, it is important to understand that the moment we were regenerated, we were sanctified through the indwelling of the Holy Spirit (John 14:7; Eph. 1:13b–14). Indeed, our bodies become the temple of the Holy Spirit (1 Cor. 6:19). And as sanctified believers we are set apart for God's service. We do not grow into sanctification. Rather we grow, develop, and serve as sanctified people.

This aspect of salvation is directly related to the principle of the priesthood of the believer and the responsibilities associated with that principle. In Jesus' magnificent prayer shortly before his arrest and trial, he says, "I sanctify myself" (John 17:19)—in other words, he dedicates himself to go to the cross so that salvation will be available to everyone. In the same way, we as priests of God are to sanctify or dedicate ourselves to the task of making known Christ's redemptive work to everyone in his name.

Third, salvation is *glorification*. The writer of Hebrews explains it this way, "So Christ was once offered to bear the sins of many; and unto them that look for him shall he appear the second time without [apart from] sin unto salvation" (Heb. 9:28). This refers to the Lord's return at the end of time as we know it. It doesn't mean that we won't know whether or not we are saved until then. Instead, the reference is to our glorification—the time of receiving our total glory and reward in heaven, including the resurrection of our bodies (cf. Rom. 8:23; Eph. 1:14).

Everyone who is regenerated will be in heaven. But our reward will be determined by the extent of our here-and-now faithfulness in sanctification (Matt. 25:14–23). Furthermore, we are assured that everyone who is in heaven will be happy, but some will enjoy a greater degree of happiness than others. Our happiness then will be determined by our faithfulness now as priests of God.

A bluegrass singer and a connoisseur of opera both attended a performance of Giacomo Puccini's *Madame Butterfly*. In many ways it was a happy experience for each of them because of their love for music. But the connoisseur of opera enjoyed the experience far more than the bluegrass singer because of his keener understanding of all that was going on.

Consequently, it isn't enough to merely get "saved" or regenerated. That is only the beginning of our spiritual pilgrimage. Sanctification is the continuing process, and glorification is the goal.

It is true that our spiritual pilgrimage involves some hardship and suffering. The apostle Paul, writing to the Christians in Colossae, mentions the price he paid to be a priest of God. He writes, "[I] now rejoice in my sufferings for you, and fill up that which is behind [lacking] of the afflictions of Christ is my flesh for his body's sake, which is the church" (Col. 1:24). Paul is saying he is happy to endure hardship and suffering as he preaches the gospel. He certainly is not saying that Christ didn't suffer enough to redeem us. Paul knew that Christ suffered redemptively for the entire human race—something impossible for Paul. But even as Christ suffered in his salvation mission, so Paul must suffer afflictions in his efforts to let everyone know about Christ's redemptive work.

A similar theme is expressed by Paul in writing to Roman Christians. "The Spirit itself beareth witness with our spirit [with us], that we are the children of God: And if children, then heirs; heirs of God, and joint-heirs with Christ; if so be that we suffer with him, that we may also be glorified together. For *I reckon that the sufferings of this present time are not worthy to be compared with the glory which shall be revealed in us*" (Rom. 8:16–18, italics mine).

In Rom. 8:17 Paul uses a play on the Greek word translated "with" as he speaks of heirs *with*, suffer *with*, and glorified *with*. Then he follows that up in v. 18 by using a bookkeeping term, "reckon" and the word "worthy," which in Greek carried the idea of scales or balances. In other words he is setting up a trial balance with a credit and a debit side in the ledger. On the debit side he enters his hardships and suffering and on the credit side he enters the glory of his (and our) future with Christ—a glory that completely outbalances any present suffering. We say that God balances the books. No, he overbalances them in our favor!

But we must not think of Christianity as simply "pie in the sky" as some non-Christians claim. We are assured of a future glory and reward. But if there were none, the Christian life is the richest and most satisfactory life on earth. And eternal life is a quality of life that begins the moment we receive Christ as Savior and continues in eternity. As believers we have abundant (overflowing) life here and now and fellowship with God and all Christians throughout all future time.

As priests of God it is our privilege to have that rich and overflowing life here, and it is our responsibility to share it with others. We enjoy the rewards of our spiritual service here and now, and we will enjoy our eternal reward and glory then and there. This means we "can have our cake and eat it too."

5. The Priesthood of the Believer and the Holy Spirit

The priesthood of the believer is intricately related to the person and work of the Holy Spirit. Indeed, apart from the Holy Spirit it would be impossible for us to understand "the deep things of God" (cf. 1 Cor. 2:10–14). Therefore, it is necessary that we examine the Holy Spirit's work in the life of the believer.

Identity of the Holy Spirit

Even though God is referred to as Father, Son, and Holy Spirit, we do not worship three Gods, but one. The writer of Deuteronomy made this clear when he said, "Hear, O Israel: The Lord our God is one Lord" (Deut. 6:4). The ancient listener and reader would have known that the Hebrew word used for God (*Elohim*) was a general term, but the Hebrew word used for Lord (*Yahweh*) referred to the one true God of Israel.

The word "trinity" does not appear in the Bible. It first appears in Christian literature in the second century A.D. The Greek *trias*, "trio" was used by Theophilus of Antioch in A.D. 181. The Latin *trinitas*, "trinity" was used first by Tertullian (A.D. 200).[1] But these words express a truth that abounds in the Bible. God is presented as one person who reveals himself as Father, Son, and Holy Spirit: three distinct persons in one, thus the triune God.

In speaking of Christ, the opening words of John's Gospel read, literally, "In the beginning always was the Word [Christ], and the Word always was equal with God, and the Word always was God himself" (John 1:1). Historically, Christ is identified with Jesus of Nazareth. John goes on to say, literally, "And the Word became flesh, and tabernacled [temporary dwelling] among us" (John 1:14). In v. 1, John uses the verb "to be" (*eimi*) to express the eternal being of Christ. But in v. 14, he uses the verb "to become" (*ginomai*) to say that the eternal Christ *became* what he had never been before, a flesh-and-blood man.

Jesus is repeatedly referred to as God. He himself said, "He that hath seen me hath seen the Father" (John 14:9), and "I and my Father are one" (John 10:30). Without protest Jesus accepted Thomas's words, "My Lord and my God" (John 20:28). And in writing to the Christians at Rome, Paul called the Holy Spirit the Spirit of God and the Spirit of Christ (Rom. 8:9).

For us, the Trinity is a mystery. But, in the Christian sense, a mystery is a truth hidden in the mind of God. It cannot be discovered or explained by human reason but must be received through divine revelation.

Many efforts have been made to explain this mystery, but none is fully satisfactory. The nearest I have come is the relationship between my wife and me before her death. I was her husband, pastor, and the father or her son—one person, but three relationships.

Dr. G. Henton Davies, Principal of Regents Park College, Oxford University, wrote that "our experience of the Holy Spirit is our experience of God in the 'gap.' "[2] For Dr. Davies, sin was the gap that separated God from human beings (cf. Isa. 59:1–8). But in Jesus Christ, God provided the means whereby people could cross over to him. And since Jesus returned to the Father, the Holy Spirit is still "God in the gap" as he seeks to lead lost people to cross over to God through faith in his Son.

The Role of the Holy Spirit

Language is a living thing and was developed through the effort of people to express life as they experienced it. For example, the biblical words for Spirit are *ruach* (Hebrew) and *pneuma* (Greek), and both literally mean wind, breath, and spirit. So, when ancient people experienced those invisible forces in nature like a breeze and a hurricane, they referred to them as *ruach* or *pneuma*.

When ancient people connected breath with living and then saw that breathing stopped when a person died, they realized they were experiencing the invisible force of life and spoke of breath as *ruach* and *pneuma*. And when they identified a spiritual but invisible inner force or drive, they spoke of this spirit as *ruach* and *pneuma*. From there they went on to associate these same words with the invisible power of God, the Spirit of God. And since God is holy, the Spirit came to be called the Holy Spirit.

In John 3:8 Jesus used a play on the word *pneuma* as both *wind* and *Spirit*. Even as we cannot see the wind, so we cannot see the Spirit, but we can see the results of their work. It makes good sense to translate this verse as "The Spirit blows [works] as he wills, and you hear the sound of it, but cannot tell whence it comes, and whither it goes: so is everyone that is born of the Spirit."

The triune God was involved in both *creation* (Gen. 1:1–2; John 1:3) and *regeneration*. The Father *proposed* it; the Son *provided* it; the Spirit *propagates* it.

The Holy Spirit is God's Spirit sent out to do God's work. In the Old Testament, the Spirit came upon people to enable them to perform special tasks for God. And when it came to the recording of the Scriptures, God's Spirit inspired those who wrote them (cf. 2 Tim. 3:16; 2 Peter 1:21).

We're told in the Gospel of Luke that the Spirit was the conceiving power in Jesus' virgin birth (Luke 1:35). At his baptism the Spirit came upon him in "bodily shape like a dove" (Luke 3:22). And Jesus received the Spirit in its fullness; he can give the Spirit to those who believe in him as Savior.

The writer of Luke's Gospel goes on to tell us that the Spirit strengthened Jesus during his wilderness temptations (Luke 4:1), and that he then returned to Galilee "in the power of the Spirit" (Luke 4:14). In Nazareth Jesus quoted Isa. 61:1–2 to show that the Spirit had anointed him for his mission (Luke 4:18–19).

All the Gospels refer to the Spirit's power in Jesus' ministry. Luke does so more than the others. The writer of Hebrews says that Jesus went to the cross in "the eternal Spirit" (9:14). And Paul wrote that Jesus was raised from the dead "in the spirit [Spirit] of holiness" (Rom. 1:4).

Furthermore, the book of Acts shows how the Spirit, after Jesus had returned to the Father, continued "all that Jesus began to do and teach" (Acts 1:1). And at Pentecost, it was the Spirit who empowered the church for its mission (Acts 2:1–4). Each new development of the spread of the gospel recorded in Acts was either at the Spirit's command or with the Spirit's approval (cf. Acts 8; 10; 13:2; 16:6–12).

Then on Paul's final trip to Jerusalem, the Spirit warned him about what would happen (Acts 21:10–14). Some people believe the Paul's imprisonment in Caesarea and Rome was punishment for disobeying the Spirit. But I'm inclined to think that those were times of preparation for the climactic moment when he was given the opportunity to preach before Caesar's tribunal.

The Holy Spirit Works with Persons

The Holy Spirit not only works in the broad arena of God's kingdom, it also works in the lives of individual persons. The Spirit convicts people of sin, righteousness, and judgment (John 16:8–11)—the sin that we all have, the righteousness that we don't have, and the judgment people face if they are outside of Christ. We need to remember that our eloquence doesn't bring conviction to one person. We give our witness; the Spirit brings conviction and also enables the convicted person to repent and believe in Jesus.

At the time of our salvation, we were "born of the Spirit" (John 3:6). The Spirit teaches, empowers, and leads us as we grow as persons and in our service for the Lord. Jesus said, "He that believeth on me, the works that I do shall he do also; and greater works than these shall he do, because I go to my Father" (John 14:12). The "greater works" are not greater in degree but in scope. And all of this is made possible through the Holy Spirit.

The Other Jesus

On the night before Jesus' crucifixion, he tried to prepare his disciples for everything that was about to happen and for their work once he had returned to the Father (John 14–17). He promised the coming of the Spirit, "And I will pray the Father, and he shall give you another Comforter, that he may abide with you forever; . . . I will not leave you comfortless [to be orphans]; I will come to you" (John 14:16, 18). You will notice that Jesus didn't tell them to pray for the Spirit. Instead, Jesus said, "*I will pray the Father*, and he shall give you another Comforter" (italics mine). Then in John 15:26 Jesus said that he would send the Spirit from the Father—further proof that he and the Father are one.

You will notice in quoting John 14:18 that after "comfortless" I put the words "to be orphans" in brackets. The Greek word used there is *orphanous*, from which we get our word orphans. Jesus was telling his disciples that he wasn't going to leave them alone or desert them. Instead he would come to them in the person of his Spirit.

And when Jesus speaks in John 14:16 of another Comforter, the Greek word used actually means "one alongside." The Latin equivalent is "advocate" (1 John 2:1). In this sense it meant a lawyer, especially a defense attorney, who stands alongside his client. The same word may also be translated counselor, paraclete, encourager, or exhorter. A more comprehensive meaning is "divine helper." But the key to v. 16 is Jesus; words, *another* Comforter, meaning another of the same kind. In other words, the Holy Spirit is another kind of helper as Jesus is. Dr. B. H. Carroll called the Spirit "the other Jesus" or "Jesus' other Self."[3]

We often think how wonderful it would have been to live with Jesus in the first century. But you and I have a greater privilege. Jesus walked alongside the apostles; his "other Self" dwells *within* us. The apostles heard Jesus speak with their ears; the Spirit whispers in *our* hearts. There were times when the apostles were out of Jesus' presence; we are never away from the Spirit's presence. The apostles were with Jesus for not more than three and one-half years; the Spirit abides with us forever.

The "other Jesus" is our guide, teacher, and helper. "But the Comforter, which is the Holy Ghost [Spirit], whom the Father will send in my name, he shall teach you all things, and bring all things to your remembrance, whatsoever I have said unto you" (John 14:26). Here is a clue to the writing of the Gospels and the interpretation of Jesus in the remainder of the New Testament (cf. John 15:26–27; 16:12–13).

Most of us find it more difficult to understand the Spirit than to understand the Father and Son. This is natural, since the Spirit does not speak of itself. Jesus said, "He shall testify of me" (John 15:26).

Furthermore, Jesus said, "He [the Spirit] shall glorify me: for he shall receive of mine, and shall shew it unto you" (John 16:14; cf. 16:13). This is a much needed word for us today.

Beware of any movement or any system of religion that magnifies the Holy Spirit above Jesus! The warning against all kinds of false teaching and false prophets is given by the writer of 1 John: "Beloved, believe not every spirit, but try [test] the spirits whether they are of God: because many false prophets are gone out into the world" (4:1). And Jesus himself warns, "And many false prophets shall rise, and shall deceive many. . . . For there shall arise false Christs, and false prophets, and shall shew great signs and wonders; insomuch that, if it were possible, they shall deceive the very elect" (Matt. 24:11, 24).

Not every so-called spiritual phenomenon is of the Holy Spirit. We should remember that the spirit of Satan as well as the Spirit of God is at work in the world. Satan's tactic is to confuse us. If he can point us away from Jesus and his redemptive work, even to the ecstatic works of the Spirit, he can wreak havoc to the cause of Christ. The important thing is that we always see the Spirit's work in relation to Jesus and his saving work. The Spirit's role is to glorify and magnify Jesus, not to detract from him.

Indwelling of the Holy Spirit

In our discussion of sanctification, I made the point that the very second we were regenerated we were sanctified—set apart as a special vessel for God's service. We were then indwelt by the Holy Spirit.

In speaking of the Spirit, Jesus says, "Whom the world cannot receive, because it seeth him not, neither knoweth him: but ye know him; for he dwelleth with you, and shall be in you" (John 14:17). In both cases the word for "know" means to *know by experience.* To speak of the Holy Spirit to non-Christians means nothing to them. It is nonsense because they have no experiential knowledge of the Spirit. But as believers we have experiential knowledge of the Spirit. And while we haven't seen the Spirit, we know by experiential knowledge the result of the Spirit's work with and in us: conviction of sin, repentance and faith, forgiveness—and *peace.*[4]

As a ten-year-old boy, I made my confession of faith in Jesus Christ in the Enon Baptist Church near Montevallo, Alabama. The preacher was Ernest Davis who later became a pastor-physician. Apparently the latter role led him to keep careful records. Years later while I was pastor of the First Baptist Church, Oklahoma City, I had the joy of visiting with him. He asked, "Would you like to know what you said to me when you came forward that day?" Of course I said that I would. He said that he asked, "Son, why are you coming today?" I replied, "Because back there [in the pew] I felt bad. I came down and now I feel good." That was my little country boy's way of saying that I had been convicted of my sin, repented, and received Christ as my Savior. And having been forgiven, I knew peace. *I felt good!* And I still do!

The indwelling Spirit is evidence that we are saved and safe. It is called the "security of the believer," or the "perseverance of the saints." This does not refer to the security of church members but of true believers.

This truth is taught throughout the New Testament. But in my judgment Paul says it best in his letter to the Ephesian Christians: "After that ye believed, *ye were sealed* with the Holy Spirit of promise, which is the *earnest* of our inheritance until the [full] redemption of the purchased possession" (Eph. 1:13b–14, italics mine).

Here we're told that the indwelling Spirit is God's seal. Historically, a seal or sign was used, among other things, for the branding of cattle or slaves or even soldiers. This meant that if cattle or slaves, for example, strayed or were stolen, proper ownership could be established. In the case of soldiers the seal was the equivalent of the modern "dog tag." It was proof of belonging. So, what Paul is saying here is the indwelling Holy Spirit—God's seal—is God's way of saying, "This one belongs to me."

This same word was used when referring to the sealing of a letter. For example, after a king wrote a letter to someone, the scroll was then rolled up and sealed with a substance like wax. The king would then imprint his signet ring in the wax, proving this was a message direct from him. In this way the seal was a guarantee of authenticity and safe delivery. Again, to bring this analogy into what Paul said, we understand that the indwelling Holy Spirit is God's guarantee of our authenticity and of our safe delivery to heaven.

There is another word of particular importance in what Paul said in Ephesians 1:13b–14, and that word is "earnest." This particular word is found only three times in the New Testament, each time in connection with the Holy Spirit (2 Cor. 1:22; 5:5; Eph. 1:14). Note that in 2 Corinthians 1:22 it is used in combination with the word "sealed."

The word "earnest" is of Semitic origin. It is a Greek transliteration of a Hebrew word meaning "pledge" (Gen. 38:17, 18, 20). In the Authorized Version of the New Testament, it is rendered by the word "earnest." However, in the more modern versions it is translated 'pledge' and 'installment' (Moffatt), 'first installment' (Williams), and 'guarantee' (RSV)." All of these translations are good. The word was used in guaranteeing the good physical condition of an animal, the validity of a title deed, and the fulfillment of a contract. It was also used in speaking of earnest money, a down payment that guarantees the full payment of something purchased.

Paul, of course, was conversant in both Hebrew and Greek. So he took this commonly used word to express an important Christian truth. Through Christ's death and resurrection God "purchased" us; this is to be the inheritance of all believers. And the Holy Spirit indwelling us is God's earnest money. In other words, God put up his very being as his guarantee to keep the believer saved and safe. And this whole transaction is the result of God's grace—a sure and certain guarantee.

On a more romantic note, the Hebrew word translated "earnest" has been used for the engagement ring the prospective groom places on the finger of the bride-to-be as a guarantee that the action will be consummated by a wedding. In this sense, we see the indwelling Holy Spirit as the engagement ring that Christ places on the finger of his bride—the church—in anticipation of John's vision of "the holy city, new Jerusalem, coming down from God out of heaven, prepared as a bride adorned for her husband" (Rev. 21:2).

In view of all of this, we can understand Paul's words and actions when he confronted certain disciples of John the Baptist in Ephesus. The King James Version has Paul asking, "Have ye received the Holy Ghost [Spirit] *since* ye believed?" (Acts 19:2, italics mine). But the literal reading of the Greek text is, "Did you receive the Holy Spirit *when* you believed?" (italics mine). Actually, he was asking them if they were saved, for in another place Paul said, "Now if any man have not the Spirit of Christ, he is none of his" (Rom. 8:9).

When these people responded that they had never even heard of the Holy Spirit, Paul preached the Good News of Jesus Christ to them, they were saved, and the Holy Spirit "came on them" (Acts 19:2–6).

Filled With the Holy Spirit

Paul exhorted the Christians at Ephesus, "Be not drunk with wine, wherein is excess, but be filled with the Spirit" (Eph. 5:18). Dr. J. B. Phillips's interpretative translation is helpful, "don't get your stimulus from wine (for there is always the danger of excessive drinking), but let the Spirit stimulate your souls."

In recent years we have heard less about the "cocktail hour" and more about the "happy hour." But alcohol only gives a temporary "lift" or stimulation, then it depresses, and there is the every-present danger of overindulgence. But Paul is saying here that the Christian is to be stimulated by the Holy Spirit. Our permanent lift and glow of personality (soul) comes by being filled with the Spirit.

Our present purpose, however, runs even deeper. What is the difference between being *indwelt* with the Spirit and being *filled* with the Spirit? Every Christian is indwelt with the Spirit. But being filled with the Spirit suggests something more, that is, the power in Christian service.

For example, a building may be filled with electricity through its wiring system. But for its power to be seen and felt it requires instruments through which it can work: bulbs, motors, etc. In a similar way, we may be indwelt with the Holy Spirit, but in order for the Spirit's power to work in and through us, certain "instruments" will be required to express it.

Many years ago the First Baptist Church in Oklahoma City hosted a citywide lay evangelism institute. The primary emphasis was on the Holy Spirit in evangelism. For several weeks after the institute a group of men met weekly for a fellowship luncheon during which we prayed and shared experiences. One day a physician shared this experience with us: "I have always tried to give a Christian witness to my patients. But most of the time I simply had to inject it unnaturally. Since attending this institute it seems to fit naturally into the conversation. I do not understand the difference unless it is that the Holy Spirit knows that now I am available." Every "priest" should be available for the Spirit to express its power freely.

Gifts of the Holy Spirit

In our work for the Lord, the Spirit has given each of us certain spiritual gifts. These gifts are more than natural talents, even though natural talents may be involved. Paul writes that the Spirit distributes these gifts "to every man [person] severally as he will" (1 Cor. 12:11). We are not to pray for certain gifts we think we'd like to have (for instance, speaking in tongues). Instead we're told that the Spirit bestows the various gifts "as he will."

But instead of using these gifts for their intended purpose, the Christians in Corinth had turned them into a source of controversy. Each person insisted that his or her gift was more important than others. Paul addresses this problem in 1 Corinthians 12–14. In chap. 12 he gives two lists of these gifts (verses 8–10, 28–30; cf. Rom. 12:6–8). While there is some duplication, different gifts are included in each list.

Using the body as an example, Paul shows the importance of each gift if the body of Christ is to function effectively (1 Cor. 12:12–27). First, he insists that these gifts are to be exercised in Christian love (agapē) (1 Cor. 12:12–27). Then in chap. 14, Paul contrasts prophecy and tongues, or languages, showing that prophecy (preaching) is more important.

Perhaps I ought to insert some comments here about "tongues." The first mention of this gift is at Pentecost (Acts 2:4–7). The Greek word for "tongues" is glōssa. Depending upon the context, it may mean the organ of speech, a specific language, or this special gift. At Pentecost Jews and Jewish proselytes were present from sixteen parts of the

Roman Empire (Acts 2:5, 9–11). Few of them spoke Aramaic, the language of Palestine at that time. So the Spirit gave the apostles (possibly others) the gift of tongues, or languages. So that "every man heard them [the disciples] speak in his own language" or "dialect." Not only did they hear the gospel in their own tongue (*glōssa*), but in their own particular dialect "wherein we were born" (Acts 2:6, 8).

Interpreters differ as to the nature of the "tongues" used in Corinth. Some believe it was a heavenly language. But along with others, I see it as the same circumstance as at Pentecost. In some way, though, the Corinthians were abusing the gift of tongues, even as they were with other gifts of the Spirit.

Since Corinth was the commercial capital of the Roman Empire, people from many different provinces of the empire came there for business reasons. This simply means that if the Spirit gave this gift of languages anywhere other than in Jerusalem at Pentecost, it seems that Corinth would be the most likely place. One thing is certain: in the New Testament the gift of tongues is always associated with evangelism. So, if visitors to Corinth heard the gospel in their own language, they could then witness to the Good News of salvation to their own people.

By the end of the first century, Christianity had spread northward into Europe so that people could preach and be heard in their own native tongues. It seems, therefore, that by that time this gift was no longer needed.

A lady is said to have criticized evangelist Dwight L. Moody for using bad grammar in his sermon. He replied, "Well, Madam, you seem to use grammar well enough. What are you doing with it for the Lord?"

This applies to every "priest" of God. Instead of fretting over the nature of "tongues," we should use the tongue or language we know and understand fulfilling our priesthood.

Fruit of the Spirit

While Paul gave more time and space to the Corinthians' problems concerning spiritual gifts, his real treatment of the more normal work of the Spirit in Christian lives is found in his letter to the church at Rome (chap. 8). The letter, incidentally, was written from Corinth. What he says there is important. Of equal interest is what he does not say. In Romans 8, he does not mention speaking in tongues, miracle healings, or other ecstatic gifts.

Paul's letter to the Galatian Christians has been referred to as a "mini-Romans." It is likely it was written from Corinth as well, either just before or just after the book of Romans. While in the Galatian letter Paul speaks of matters not found in Romans, the theme is largely that of the Romans letter in miniature. Of particular interest at this point are Paul's words about "the fruit of the Spirit" (Gal. 5:22–23). Note the singular "fruit" like a cluster of grapes: "love, joy, peace, long-suffering, gentleness, goodness, faith, meekness, temperance [self-control]." Each of these is an inner grace, and there is no reference to ecstatic activity.

As we strive to fulfill our role as believer-priests, we will do well to major in the inner graces. When the beauty of Jesus can be seen in us, our neighbors across the street and across the world will see the difference he makes in our lives.

6. The Priesthood of the Believer and Ministry

In the priesthood of the believer role there must be a balance between privilege and responsibility. It is always a temptation to stress the privilege and minimize the responsibility. And most certainly the privileges stretch our imaginations. The writer of Exodus had this to say, "Now therefore *if* ye will obey my voice indeed and keep my covenant, *then* ye shall be a peculiar treasure unto me above all people . . . and ye shall be unto me a kingdom of priests" (Exod. 19:5–6a, italics mine). But even as we stress the "*then* ye shall be unto me a kingdom of priests," we must never forget the "if ye will obey my voice."

Consequently, we now turn our attention to the responsibilities associated with our priesthood. And another word for responsibilities is "ministry." This is our mission in life as Christians.

Meaning of Ministry

Unfortunately, most of the time we associate the word "ministry" with the ordained clergy. We speak of someone being called into ministry—a full-time religious vocation. I believe that God does call people to specific ministries, even as Jesus called the disciples. But to limit God's call to ministry to ordained people is to ignore the fact that *all* believers are called to serve the Lord even though they may be involved in some other vocation.

It is an old but meaningful story. A shoe cobbler was asked as to the nature of his business. He replied, "Serving the Lord." When pressed for more specifics, he said, "My business is serving the Lord. But I peg shoes to pay expenses."

The Greek noun for "minister" is *diakonos*. Literally, it means "through dust." The exact derivation of the word is uncertain. Dr. A. T. Robertson suggests the idea of a slave raising dust in his haste to obey his owner.[1] The usual word for a slave or bond servant is *doulos*. It was Paul's favorite term of self-designation (see Rom. 1:1).

But *diakonos* denoted the lowest order of slaves—the ones who were called upon to perform the most menial of tasks. This word is used thirty times in the King James Version of the New Testament. Twenty times it is translated "minister," seven times as "servant," and three times as "deacon" (Phil. 1:1; 1 Tim. 3:8, 12). But "minister" does not connote "The Reverend John Doe." Rather, it suggests the role of a servant.

The Greek word for "ministry" is *diakonia* and is found sixteen times in the New Testament. It does not refer to a separate class of Christians but to the type of service to be performed by all believers in Christ. All Christians as slaves of Jesus Christ are to be involved in ministry.

The complex life of present-day churches necessitates professional church staffs of varying sizes. Too often the idea prevails, though, that they are paid to do the Lord's work. As with the Levites in Israel, they should be supported financially by those *with* whom they serve. Notice that I said "with" not "for," or in the place of others. No matter how much we pay them, we cannot pay them enough to do *our* work for the Lord—ministering is every Christian's job!

Model in Ministry

As Christians, we are to pattern our lives after the life of Jesus. Every Christian should be Christlike. Therefore, Jesus Christ is our model in ministry.

It is a tragedy to see followers of "the lowly Jesus" striving for position in the Lord's work. But this was the case even among the apostles. Before Christ's death and resurrection and the coming of the Holy Spirit at Pentecost, the apostles assumed Jesus would set up an earthly kingdom. They often debated which of them should be the greatest in his kingdom.

Perhaps the lowest note struck in this rivalry was sounded when the disciples and Jesus were headed for Jerusalem just before his death. Apparently in an attempt to coerce Jesus into telling them what their payoff for service would be, Peter said, with an obvious note of self-righteousness, "Lo, we have left all, and have followed thee" (Mark 10:28). In response Jesus assured his disciples that anyone who left everything and served him would be rewarded, but then he went on to describe what was going to happen to him when they arrived in Jerusalem: he would be arrested, tortured, and condemned to death—the price of their salvation (Mark 10:32–34).

But Jesus' listeners didn't hear what he was saying, and they missed the point entirely. We next read that James and John approached Jesus quietly and asked a favor. And when he asked what they wanted, " [T]hey said to him, grant unto us that we may sit, one on thy right hand, and the other on the left hand, in thy glory" (Mark 10:35–37). They wanted to sit in the places of highest honor, and we're next told that when the other disciples heard what James and John had asked for, they were "much displeased." It is interesting, though, the disciples were disturbed not because they thought the request of James and John was wrong. Rather, they were "much displeased" because James and John had beaten them to the punch.

There's more behind this story than appears on the surface. In narrating this same story, the writer of Matthew tells us that James and John's mother was involved in their request. Their mother, Salome, was evidently Mary's sister, Jesus' aunt. From this we get the picture: Aunt Salome and cousins James and John were trying to trade on the family relationship. In effect, they were suggesting that the power base of Jesus' kingdom *be kept in the family*.

Kindly but firmly Jesus lets James and John and all of the other disciples know just how impossible the request is (Mark 10:38–40). Then he moves on to show them the true sign of greatness in his kingdom: "Ye know that they which are accounted to rule over the Gentiles exercise lordship over them; and their great ones exercise authority over them. But so shall it not be among you: but whosoever will be great among you, shall be your minister; And whatsoever of you will be the chiefest, shall be servant of all. For even the Son of man came not to be ministered unto, but to minister, and to give his life a ransom for many [all]" (Mark 10:42–45).

Literally, Jesus is saying that the Gentile or pagan rulers lord it over and tyrannize their subjects. But that is *not* the Christian standard because Christian greatness is based on service—to "minister" is to "serve." Jesus didn't come into the world so that others could render menial service to him. Rather, he came to serve others—even to the point of dying for their sins.

The contrast is vivid. Secular society judges greatness by the number of people who serve a person. But the Lord determines our greatness by the number of people *we* serve. Jesus is the perfect model of true greatness. Consequently, he is our model for ministry.

The writer of John's Gospel gives us a colorful example of this (John 13:2–10). It was the custom of that time for a servant (minister) to rinse the road dust from the feet of arriving guests. In this story the twelve disciples and Jesus are in the Upper Room. There was no servant to cleanse the guests' feet, so Jesus, the host, took on the task himself.

Immediately, Peter protested, "Thou shalt never wash my feet." Peter was embarrassed. He knew that none of the status-seeking disciples, including himself, would wash each other's feet like a common servant, and he didn't want his Lord to do it either. But Jesus made it clear that if Peter wouldn't let Jesus wash him, he couldn't be a part of the group. Then in classic style, Jesus drove his point home, "If I then your Lord and Master, have washed your feet; ye also ought to wash one another's feet" (John 13:14). As priest-ministers of Christ, our task is to serve.

Equipped for Ministry

It is customary to refer to Jesus' entrance into Jerusalem on what we call Palm Sunday as his "triumphant entry." But there is a vivid contrast between Jesus' entry to Jerusalem on that day and the triumphant entry of a victorious king or general to his capital city after a successful war campaign. At such a moment of triumph the victor rode a white stallion and paraded proudly through the streets. Tagging along behind in chains was the defeated king or general. As they moved through the crowds, the people shouted the victor's praises and threw flowers on him; he in return threw coins into the crowd.

Jesus' entry in Jerusalem on that Sunday had none of these features. This was *before the battle,* not after the victory. And he rode a donkey as did a king in those days when he visited one of the cities in his realm in times of peace and tranquility. Jesus' entry into the city of Jerusalem that day might better be called his "royal entry," for he came offering peace to the city and her people.

Perhaps Paul discusses Jesus' triumphant entry well in his letter to the Ephesian Christians, "Wherefore, he saith, When he ascended up on high, he led captivity captive, and gave gifts to men" (Eph. 4:8). What were the gifts Jesus gave to the world? Paul answers, "And he gave some, apostles; and some, prophets; and some, evangelists; and some, pastors and teachers" (Eph. 4:11).

The apostles were the missionaries, the ones sent forth to take the Good News of salvation through Christ to people who hadn't heard it before (cf. Rom 5:19–20).   The prophets were proclaimers of truth to their contemporaries; they were forth-tellers as well as foretellers. In the New Testament the greater emphasis is upon preaching the gospel with power like an evangelist. And the pastors and teachers were the leaders in the individual churches. They were the ones who nurtured the Christians: "For the perfecting of the saints, for the work of the ministry, for the edifying of the body of Christ" (Eph. 4:12).

Since there was no punctuation in Greek except the question mark, the punctuation in Ephesians 4:12 was arbitrary. It becomes clearer and more accurate if we translate it this way, "For the perfecting [equipping] of the saints [Christians] for the work of ministry, with a view to building up the body of Christ."

The task then of the pastors and teachers is to equip Christians (saints) to do the work of ministry, and the goal is the building up of the body of Christ, the church. The point is important. All believer-priests are called to nurture and equip each other for Christian witness. It isn't the job of just one kind of Christian. Rather, it is everybody working together in harmony that gets the job done.

Here is a true story. In one of our southern cities the most rapidly growing church is a Methodist church. From all over the city, young people flock to it. Because many Baptists were deserting their churches, a disturbed group of Baptist pastors asked this Methodist pastor what he was doing to create so much excitement.

The Methodist pastor said, "We found an old book on how to grow a Sunday school written by Arthur Flake. We studied it, taught it to our people, and are following it to the letter."

Ironically, Arthur Flake was a Baptist, employed by the Southern Baptist Sunday School Board. As part of his work many years ago, he wrote what perhaps is the greatest book ever written on growing a Sunday school. And, of course, Southern Baptists are strong on the idea that great churches are grown through great Sunday schools.

Arthur Flake's book has been out of print for many years. And most of the new generation of Southern Baptists don't know about it. But this Methodist pastor had stumbled onto a copy. And he is using it with astounding success. He *was* a wise pastor and teacher who was willing to use every tool possible—even a Baptist book—to nurture and equip his members to bring people to the Lord. And new converts are nurtured and equipped to minister.

Motive for Ministry

What should be our motive in ministry? To get more people into our churches? No! To increase the financial offerings? No! To gain the gratitude of people? No! To discharge our obligation to minister? No! These are results, not motives worthy of our calling. What then is the Christian motive for ministry? It is Christian love (*agapē*)!

It was out of God's love that he gave his Son as our Savior. It was this love that led Jesus to the cross. And it is his love for us and our love for him that leads us to love those for whom he died. "Hereby perceive we the love of God, because he laid down his life for us: and we ought to lay down our lives for the brethren" (1 John 3:16). The word "brethren" refers to fellow Christians. But, if we love as God loves, we will also love the unsaved (cf. Rom. 5:8). We may not like some people and the way they live, but in the sense of *agapē*, we can love them. It has been said many times, but it is still true: God hates sin, but he loves the sinner. And this is our guideline as priests of God.

Now, when Christians stop *really* loving people, something within them dies. This truth was illustrated over and over again in the experience of ancient Israel. And the book of Hebrews, especially, makes it clear this can happen to Christians as well. Many Bible interpreters understand the book of Hebrews as a warning to Hebrew Christians against rejecting Christ and returning to Judaism, an action that would cause them to lose their salvation. But I want to explore what I think is a better interpretation.

We don't know who wrote the book of Hebrews, but several different writers have been suggested, including Paul, Apollos, and Barnabas. We have no clues, however, in the writing itself. The style of the book reflects the Alexandrian (Egypt) school of thought, a style that used the allegorical method of interpretation. This pattern fits both Apollos and

Barnabas. Personally, I opt for Barnabas because his name literally means "son of exhortation." Luke identifies the meaning of his name in Acts 4:36 as "son of consolation," however, the word "consolation" may also read "exhortation." For me this is significant because Hebrews contains five exhortation verses (2:13; 3:7–19; 6:1–16; 10:19–31; 12:1–2). This style seems to point toward Barnabas.

I believe the writer of Hebrews uses the allegorical method in interpreting the historical Exodus events—Israel's redemption from Egyptian bondage and all that transpired in the years that followed before they entered Canaan. And with this in mind the author of Hebrews warns his Christian readers not to let happen to them what had happened to their ancestors.

To understand this better, we will take a closer look at Hebrews 6:1–6, perhaps one of the most difficult passages in the Bible to interpret. However, I suggest you turn in your Bibles and read Numbers 13–14.

As we have seen, three months after the people of Israel had left Egypt, Moses led them to Mount Sinai. It was there that God and the Israelites entered into a conditional covenant whereby Israel would be a kingdom of priests whose task was to lead their pagan neighbor-nations to worship the Lord God. And as a base for their operation God promised to give them the land of Canaan.

Two years after their escape from Egypt, the Israelites arrived at Kadesh-barnea, the southern gateway into Canaan. From there Moses sent twelve men to spy on the land (Numbers 13). When the spies returned to camp, they brought a glowing report about the wonders of the land, but ten of them said it would be impossible to conquer it because of the walled cities and the powerful giants who occupied them. The minority report was given by Caleb and Joshua who insisted that with God's help they could overcome the enemy.

The people accepted the majority report and refused to move forward into Canaan. They not only rebelled against God, they also discussed the possibility of selecting a new leader to replace Moses and then head back south and east to Egypt. But God wouldn't permit the return of his redeemed people to Egypt, and as punishment for their rebellion the Lord said that all Israelites over nineteen years of age, except Caleb and Joshua, would spend the rest of their lives in the wilderness desert. Only after their death would God permit his people to move into Canaan. It is important to note that the rebellion of the Israelites at Kadesh-barnea didn't defeat God's redemptive purpose. It was only delayed for a period of forty years. These rebels did not lose their redemption from Egyptian bondage, but they lost their opportunity to be a part of God's redemptive purpose.

With that in mind let us examine what the writer is saying in Hebrews 6:1–6. Note that the theme is not "Don't go back into the bondage of Egypt." Rather, it is "Let us go on unto perfection" (6:1). "Perfection" here means the fulfillment of these Hebrew Christians' purpose of being—their place in God's redemptive plan. They are urged to go beyond the elementary matters in their Christian lives into the real purpose of their being as *priests* of God (6:1–3). Then they will be "partakers of the Holy Ghost" (6:4b), partners with the Holy Spirit in God's redemptive purpose.

In Heb. 6:4–5, following the words "It is impossible," the author uses spiritual terms corresponding to the report of the Israelite spies as to the land of Canaan. He is thinking of the arrested development of his readers (cf. Heb. 5:12–6:2). Then going back and picking up "It is impossible," he adds, "If they shall fall away [rebel]—it is impossible to renew them again unto repentance" (6:6a) In other words, if they remain in this state of arrested development and failure to fulfill their obligation as Christian priests, they too will lose their opportunity to be used of God in his redemptive purpose. One thing is certain, God's purpose will succeed. But they will have no part in it because of their living desert, their barren wasted lives.

Why is it impossible for them to be renewed again unto repentance? To get the answer we return to the Israelite encampment of Kadesh-barnea (Numbers 14). After hearing the Lord condemn them to forty years of desert living because of their disobedience, the tribal leaders held a conference and decided it would be preferable to die trying to go into Canaan than to live out their lives in that desert wilderness. So the next morning they told Moses they had changed their minds and were ready to enter Canaan. But Moses said that was impossible; God had already decreed otherwise.

It helps in understanding this to know that the Greek word for repentance is *metanoia*. It comes from *meta*, which means about, and *nous*, which is mind. To the Greeks "mind" signified the total person. So *metanoia* means a change of mind or an about-face of the mind. It indicated a change of mind, heart, attitude, or a change of a person's total direction of life. With this in mind, we can now see that the people of Israel could not "repent" of their decision.

Let's take this a step further and apply it to Christians—to a Sunday school class that is made up of really nice people who love each other. These folks have a lot of fun at their parties and even look forward to Sunday simply because they enjoy just being together. They are even open-minded enough not to mind if a new person joins the class now and then—provided, of course, the new person is one of "their" kind. But the truth of the matter is they're really not concerned about people in general. They just love each other and their social club, the Sunday school class.

Then one day someone asks, "Where is Mary?" Another member says, "Didn't you hear? She died last week!" And as the years pass, they begin to realize that the undertaker is taking their class away from them. In response to that sobering fact someone says, "We have to get out and enroll some new members or our class will soon be gone!" From this we see that they're still not concerned about people; it is the Sunday school class with all its social meaning that absorbs their attention and energy.

But then comes the rude awakening: nobody wants to join their class. Word has gotten around about their attitude. Consequently, the class dwindles away and dies. Why? Because they do not love people! Their opportunity to serve God and people was lost. It can happen to a church, to a class, and even to you and me. How cautious we need to be about any attitude other than love!

Actually the theme of a lost opportunity is introduced by the writer of Hebrews in these words, "Therefore we ought to give the more earnest heed to the things which we have heard, lest at any time we should let them *slip* (2:1 italics mine). This sounds as if they were in danger of losing something. But in Greek the verb to "let slip" is passive. So, instead of these Hebrew Christians doing something to themselves, they face the danger of something being done to them.

The Greek verb translated "slip" means to flow along or flow by. It was used by the Greek historian Xenophon to describe a flowing river. Now, let's give the flowing river a Christian meaning. I see it as symbolic of God's redemptive purpose. The river flows out of eternity, through history, and then into the ocean of eternity. Those first-century Hebrew Christians were standing with their feet barely in the water. The author urges them to get out into the mainstream and go along with the river. Otherwise they *will be flowed by*. They will still be in the river, but will be left behind. They will not stop the redemptive purpose of God, but they will be flowed by as it proceeds on its way. A lost opportunity! Every priest of God should be in the mainstream of God's redemptive purpose. And the motive for being in God's mainstream must be love.

Areas of Ministry

To be in God's mainstream is to minister to and serve people. But then comes the question, "Where are we to minister?" Actually, there is more than one answer as we consider both the place and type of ministry.

First, there are *geographical* considerations. Following his resurrection Jesus gave several commissions. The final one comes to us when Jesus said this to his disciples on the Mount of Olives just prior to his ascension, "But ye shall receive power, after that the Holy Ghost [Spirit] is come upon you: and ye shall be witnesses unto me both in Jerusalem, and in all Judea, and in Samaria, and unto the uttermost part of the earth" (Acts 1:8).

Earlier Jesus had told them that he would send them the Spirit that was promised by the Father. Then he added, "But tarry ye in the city of Jerusalem, until ye be endued with power from on high" (Luke 24:49). If they attempted to minister in their own strength, they would fail. They needed the Spirit's power.

Prior to this, on resurrection Sunday night when Jesus appeared to the apostles, "breathed on them, and saith unto them, Receive ye the Holy Spirit" (John 20:22). From this we understand they were already indwelt by the Spirit. But Jesus had in mind here their being *filled* with the Spirit. And a few days later he told them to wait for the coming of the Spirit.

Dr. Robertson resolves this seeming conflict when he calls this "a foretaste of the great pentecost."[2] He points out that the Greek for the verb "receive" should actually read, "Begin to receive ye the Holy Spirit."

The writer of the Gospel of Luke recorded that Jesus told his disciples to wait in Jerusalem until the Spirit came in power (24:49). But, they were not merely to sit and wait for this to happen. The Greek verb translated "be endured" calls for a passive—the subject is acted upon. In Greek, however, the construction is "reflexive," that is, it implies something done within the disciples themselves. With this in mind, the phrase should actually read, "until you get yourselves clothed with power from on high." In other words, the disciples were to prepare themselves to receive the Spirit's power when the Spirit came. We understand that the Holy Spirit had been at work in the world from the beginning. But now the Spirit was coming in a special way to propagate the gospel proposed by the Father and provided by the Son. And the Spirit would do this through believers, the priests of God.

What were Jesus' disciples doing during this ten-day waiting period between Jesus' Ascension and Pentecost? We know they were praying (Acts 1:14)—not only the disciples but other Christians had joined with them in prayer. When Christians pray together, they come together. So we may well imagine that they were confessing their sins to God and asking for his forgiveness. Also they were confessing wrongs doe to each other and forgiving one another.

Differences between believers and God, between believers and each other sap spiritual strength. But the disciples during that ten-day period were together with one heart and will. So when the Spirit came in power they were ready—in one spirit and with one purpose.

At the same time Jesus gave the disciples the promise of the Spirit's power, he told them where they were to minister. They were to begin where they were (Jerusalem), move into nearby areas (Judea), then father out (Samaria), until they had reached the last part of the earth. The New American Bible reads "even to the remotest part of the earth." This simple means that as long as there is one place where the gospel has not been preached and/or one person who has not heard it, we are to keep going until Jesus returns.

Realistically, of course, everyone cannot go everywhere. But wherever we are, we are to give our witness for Christ—both by word and by deed. And where we cannot go, we are to help send those whom the Lord has called to minister elsewhere.

Most certainly, the apostle Paul in his time modeled for us Jesus' instructions about being his witnesses "in Jerusalem, and in all Judea, and in Samaria, and unto the uttermost part of the earth" (Acts 1:8b). In writing to the Christians in Rome, Paul said "from Jerusalem, and round about unto Illyricum [across the Adriatic Sea from Italy], I have fully preached the gospel of Christ" (Rom. 15:9). He is saying that up to that time he had started a ring of churches around the northern part of the Mediterranean. And in doing this he had witnessed to the gospel to people who have never heard it before (Rom. 15:20). He goes on to say that his goal is to take the gospel to Spain on the western end of the known world.

It was said of the Straits of Gibraltar that *ne plus ultra*—no more beyond. It wasn't until well over a thousand years later that people knew there was any "more beyond" to the west, and they dropped the *ne*, leaving *plus ultra*—more beyond. Those words should be the slogan of every priest of God, for as long as there is one person on this earth that has not heard about Christ, our task is unfinished.

Reflecting further on the words of Jesus in Acts 1:8, we discover another interesting thing. We're told that as Jesus and the apostles were on their way to the Mount of Olives, the place of his ascension, they "began and continued to ask" Jesus if at that time he was going to restore the kingdom to Israel. This, of course, involved Jesus' second coming.

Finally, Jesus said, "It is not for you to know the times or the seasons [points and periods, fine details], which the Father hath put in his own power [*exousia*, authority]" (Acts 1:17). Immediately after saying that he continued, "but," and the rest of v. 8 contains Jesus' commission. The word "but" sets the thought in v. 8 over against that in v. 7. In short, Jesus said, "You leave with God that which is his business alone. And you get busy doing what by God's grace is your business alone—evangelizing and ministering to a lost and suffering world."

In addition to the geographical area of ministry, there is the *spiritual area.* Any work of the Lord is spiritual. But I use the term here as referring to the deepest needs of the human heart. This directs us to an examination of what we call the Great Commission (Matt. 28:18–20).

First, though, we need to understand that the commission to go and teach and baptize was not given only to the disciples. The writer of Matthew says others were involved, "And when they saw him they worshipped him: but some doubted" (Matt. 28:17). Who were these doubters of Jesus' bodily resurrection? Surely not the apostles, for they had seen him alive since that event. Apparently, the reference here is other believers in Galilee who had accompanied the apostles to the place where Jesus gave the Great Commission. They may well be the "above five hundred brethren" Paul mentions in 1 Cor. 15:6. But whoever they were, they were doubters until assured that Jesus was really alive. Then they believed all the more. This means that the Great Commission was given to believers in general—to all Christians.

Jesus' first words in his Great Commission are "All power [authority] is given unto me in heaven and in earth." This was the authority of the resurrected Lord (Matt. 28:18). Then after affirming his authority, he says, "Go ye therefore, and teach all nations, baptizing them in the name of the Father, and of the Son, and of the Holy Ghost" (Matt. 28:19). We think of the word "go" as an imperative, a command, but it is actually a participle going or as you go. Jesus here didn't *command* his disciples to go. He never entertained the idea that they would do anything else with the good news of salvation. Of course they would go and share it with people everywhere.

The only imperative in the Greek version of that verse is the word "teach." Literally Jesus said, "as you go, disciple all nations." The word "disciple" means to enroll everybody to be Jesus' pupils. Then, having enrolled them, they were to baptize them and teach them "to observe all things whatsoever I [Jesus] have commanded you" (Matt. 28:20). These last words are important. Most of us do a better job of making disciples and baptizing them than we do in *teaching* them. Someone has wisely said, "The process of evangelism is not complete until the evangelized become evangelists."

Then comes the great promise, "Lo, I am with you alway, even unto the end of the world" (Matt. 28:20b) Literally translated, this reads, "I am with you all the days until the final consummation of the age." Notice the words, "all days." That means good days and bad days, days of joy and days of sorrow, days of victory and days of defeat—it includes them all. He is with us *all days* in the presence and power of his Holy Spirit.

I've heard Christians say they do not witness to others about Jesus out of fear they will fail. Here is some good news—there is no way we can fail when we tell others about the Lord. For in the act of witnessing, we have succeeded. Remember, we are not the judge, jury, or the prosecuting attorney. We are witnesses. Of course we are to pray for those who don't know Christ. But once we have witnessed to them, we've done all we can. The rest is between them and the Lord.

After the geographical and spiritual areas of ministry comes the *fellowship area.* As priests of God we are responsible for one another. We are to "lift up the hands which hang down, and the feeble knees;And make straight paths for your feet, lest that which is lame be turned out of the way, but rather let it be healed" (Heb. 12:12–13).

In Ephesians, following the verse about equipping the saints for ministry, Paul says, "Till we all come in the unity of the faith, and of the [full] knowledge of the Son of God, unto a perfect [mature, adult] man, unto the measure of the stature of the fullness of Christ" (Eph. 4:13; see also 4:14–16). We need each other, and we are to support and nurture our fellow Christians.

Finally, our ministry includes the *social area.* We are to witness to a spiritual gospel, which has social implications. We are to minister to the needy and unfortunate both within and *outside* the Christian fellowship (cf. Acts 4:34–37; 2 Corinthians 8–9). While Jesus did not say so, the implication is that the good Samaritan was a Christian. Otherwise a Samaritan would not have ministered to a Jew.

In the parable of the last judgment Jesus laid down this principle: we ourselves are judged by how we treat unfortunate people (Matt. 25:31–46). In this story, Jesus identifies himself with them. We understand that in ministering to them, we minister to him. And failure to minister to the hungry, the thirsty, the poor is failure to serve the Lord.

This is not to say that we can be saved simply by performing good deeds; the final judgment will not decide who is saved and lost. It will declare it. It will show the kind of character we bring to the judgment. We serve and help others because we are children of God. Failing to do that reveals that we are not his children (cf. Matt. 25:45–46).

Fruit and Reward in Ministry

The fruit, or results, of our ministry as priests of God will be the people that have been saved through our witness. The reward of our ministry will be, not only the joy of serving, but the commendation of the Savior whose we are and whom we serve (Matt. 25:34). We are not to minister simply for reward and glory. But we may be certain that the God who calls us to serve will not let us go unrewarded. And in that glorious future day we will desire nothing more than his smile of approval.

7. The Priesthood of the Believer and the Church

The word "church" is a commonly used word today. It appears one hundred and fifteen times in the New Testament. But according to the record in the Gospels, Jesus only used it three times (Matt. 16:18; 18:17).

The Greek word translated "church" is *ekklēsia,* a compound of *ek,* meaning "out of" and the verb *kaleō,* which means I call. So the church is the "called-out ones." In some places this same word is translated "assembly" (Acts 19:41). To complete the picture, the church is people called out of their homes and or businesses to assemble together.

In A.D. 29, Jesus led the apostles on a series of four withdrawals from Galilee. These extended from the time of the Passover until shortly before the Feast of Tabernacles. During this time, he taught the Twelve intensely. They were in the fourth of these, withdrawals near Caesarea Philippi, when Jesus asked the apostles who they thought he was. Peter replied for the group, "Thou art the Christ, the Son of the living God" (Matt. 16:16).

After pronouncing a blessing upon Peter for his witness, Jesus said, "Thou art Peter, and upon this rock I will build my church; and the gates of hell [Hades] shall not prevail against it. And I will give unto thee the keys of the kingdom of heaven: and whatsoever thou shalt bind on earth shall be bound in heaven: and whatsoever thou shalt loose on earth shall be loosed in heaven" (Matt. 16:18–19). Earlier we commented on 19 in a different connection. Now we will examine it as part of a whole in relationship to the church.

Foundation of the Church

"Thou art Peter, and upon this rock I will build my church." Who or what is the foundation of the church? Since Jesus spoke directly to Peter, "You are Peter," some believe that he is the foundation. However, we have an alternative. When Peter made his confession about Jesus, he spoke for the Twelve. Such being the case, it is possible to think that Jesus was speaking to the Twelve through Peter.

Still others see the foundation as Peter's confession of faith along with everyone who echoes his confession. But there is one compelling reason why none of these is true. It is found in the language Jesus used.

The word "Peter" translates the Greek word *petros*. It is masculine gender. Jesus said that "upon this rock I will build my church." "Rock" translates *petra*, which is feminine gender. So the two cannot mean the same thing.

Petra denotes a large foundation stone. *Petros* means a small stone broken off a *petra* and partaking of its nature. This is the relationship Peter and we have to Christ.

There are those who believe that Peter was the head of the apostles. But that is based upon tradition, not upon Scripture. It is true that Peter spoke for the apostles, but that was because of his outspoken nature. But it is also true that his habit of speaking out got him into hot water at times (Luke 22:31–34). We know the apostles didn't think of Peter as being their head or leader because of their constant squabble as to which one of them would be greatest in Jesus' kingdom. We also know that Paul did not regard Peter as the head of the apostles. As an apostle, he had a heated confrontation with Peter in Antioch (Gal. 2:11). But most convincing evidence is Peter himself, in writing to elders, identified himself simply as an elder among elders, not a super-elder (1 Pet. 5:1).

The head of the apostles and the foundation of the church is Jesus Christ (1 Cor. 3:11). And Christians as living stones are

being built up as a "spiritual house," the foundation of which
is Christ (1 Pet. 2:5). In writing to the Colossian Christians,
Paul insists that "he [Christ] is head of the body, the church"
(Col. 1:18).

The Nature of the Church

As we take a close look at the nature of the church, I may
seem to belabor or place undue emphasis on certain words and
phrases. But follow me closely because the point I am making is
most important.

In English we place emphasis by the inflection of the voice.
For instance, "I will *build* my church," or "I will build my
church." But in Greek emphasis is determined by the position
of a word or phrase in a sentence. For instance, when a noun
and a pronoun are used together, the emphasis is on the one
which precedes the other. This is the case here. The pronoun
precedes the noun. With this understanding, Jesus is speaking
of the "me, church" or "my church." This suggests that there
were other kinds of churches, or *ekklēsias*.

In the Greek translation of the Old Testament (known as the
Septuagint), *ekklēsia* is used to translate the Hebrew word *qahal*.
This word referred to the congregation of Israel (all of God's
people) assembled before God and under his direct theocratic
rule. This suggests the *general* idea of the church as being all of
the redeemed in all time.

Among the Greeks, *ekklēsia* was used in the political sense. In
the Roman Empire, some cities were designated as "free" cities.
This was done as a reward for some special service to the Empire. It involved such things as exemption from certain taxes
and the right of local democratic rule. But that rule had to be
within the framework of the laws of the Empire.

Ephesus was a free city. In Acts 19, Luke records the riot scene
in the arena in Ephesus. When finally the "townclerk" (19:35),
who presided at such meetings, got control of the situation,
he reminded the mob that such matters could be settled in a

"lawful assembly" (19:39). Luke then added, "And when he had thus spoken, he dismissed the assembly" (19:41). In both of these verses, the word "assembly" translates *ekklēsia*. So in this instance we see a local body of citizens operating through democratic processes within the framework of the laws of the Roman Empire.

In effect, Jesus was saying, "The Hebrews have their *ekklēsia*, and the Greeks have their *ekklēsia*. Now I will build *my ekklēsia* (Matt. 16:18). The word "church" is used in both ways in the New Testament. A few times it refers to the church as the body of Christ consisting of everyone in all time who has been saved through faith in Christ (cf. Eph. 1:22–23; Col. 1:18). In this sense, the church is a theocracy under God's direct rule. But in ninety-three out of one hundred and fifteen times *ekklēsia* appears in the New Testament, it refers to *local* churches. The singular form is never used of a group of churches or a denomination. Where more than one church is involved, the plural is used (cf. 2 Cor. 8:1; Gal. 1:2). So in light of the Greek idea, we may define a local New Testament church as a local body of baptized believers operating through democratic processes under the lordship of Jesus Christ. Of Jesus' three uses of *ekklēsia*, one refers to the church in the general, or institutional sense (Matt. 16:18), while the other two speak of the local church (Matt. 18:17).

Now, when we refer to the autonomy of the local church, we don't mean that it can do as it pleases. The local, or individual church must do as Christ pleases or wills, and this also applies to each person in the local church. To do as we please is not autonomy but anarchy. We must be careful not to confuse our wills with God's will.

From this analysis it is clear that the church is both an absolute monarchy and a pure democracy. This is a paradox, to be sure. And yet there is unity in this diversity.

In proclaiming Christ as Lord, the believer belongs to an absolute monarchy (Matt. 28:18; Rev. 17:14). While it is true that he is in heaven, yet he relates himself to his subjects through his revealed Word and through his Holy Spirit. Christ our king does not delegate his authority through any individual or group. His dealings are directly with individual persons. And at the earthly level, Christ's lordship is expressed in granting church autonomy *under* his lordship. Consequently, he recognizes the personhood and responsible freedom of *every* believer.

It is this responsible freedom that calls for democracy in the local church. But it is a freedom under the lordship of Christ. Such churches are held together through a common faith in our Lord and mutual dedication to a common task and a common goal, both of which are assigned to us by our reigning Lord.[1]

In the church, we are involved in fellowship, not membership: We speak of church membership, but the New Testament speaks of fellowship, *koinōnia* (Acts 2:42). A little boy defined fellowship as two fellows in the same ship. That isn't a bad definition. For *koinōnia* means a sharing or having things in common. When Paul spoke of the Philippian church having "fellowship in the gospel" (Phil. 1:5), he referred to monetary gifts sent to him. They shared in his work as he preached the gospel. The writer of 1 John speaks of others having "fellowship with us, and truly our fellowship is with the Father, and with his Son Jesus Christ" (1:3; see also 1:6–7). Here the writer is speaking of Christian relationships.

Church fellowship involves more than church membership. You can be a *member* simply by having your name on the church roll, even though you may never attend, participate in church activities, or provide financial support. But *fellowship* means being involved in all that the church family is doing.

In his book, Dr. E. Y. Mullins's third axiom is "All Believers Have a Right to Equal Privileges in the Church."[2] This calls for democracy in church government. But over against the privilege we must set the responsibility. The priesthood of the believer involves both. The New Testament knows nothing about spectator or sponge religion. As priests, we should not sit in the stands and watch the game. We should be in the game.

When the writer of Hebrews refers to the "cloud of witnesses" (*marturōn*), he isn't thinking of spectators viewing the relay race (12:1). Rather, the "witnesses" are the ones listed in Hebrews 11, and others like them, who have successfully run their part of the race and are watching us as we run ours.

At the end of that marvelous "faith chapter," the writer says, *"that they without us should not be made perfect"* (Heb. 11:40, italics mine). The words "be made perfect" translate a Greek verb that means to complete a task, to achieve the final goal. In other words, those who went before us have successfully run their part of the race. But the total race will not be won unless we who follow them win our segment. This holds true until the end of time at the Lord's return. They have passed the torch on to us. So "let us lay aside every weight, and the sin which doth so easily beset us, and let us run with patience the race that is set before us" (Heb. 12:1).

This race metaphor is very descriptive because nothing could slow them down or hinder their progress. This is a colorful picture of how we are to "run the Christian race." We are to rid ourselves of any besetting sin and run with patience. In Greek the word for "patience" means "an abiding under." It was used in athletic and military life for one who could endure all that his opponent threw at him, yet have reserve strength with which to countercharge to victory.

The Greek word for "race" is *agōna,* from which our word agony comes. We are to agonize as we pay the price for victory. We are to do this, not for the cheers of the crowd, but "looking unto Jesus the author and finisher [pioneer and goal] of our faith, who for the joy that was set before him endured the cross, despising the shame, and is set down at the right hand of the throne of God" (Heb. 12:2). From God's throne on high Jesus, too, is watching us as we run our part of the race. If we are to rejoice in his final, complete victory, we must pay the price in suffering and dedication (Rom. 8:17–18).

Church fellowship calls for our cooperation. Experience has taught us that what we do best is that which we do together. Yet in group activities there are times when not every participant gets his or her way. This is where fellowship takes over. Insofar as opportunity allows, we should cooperate at the planning stage. Along with all others "speaking the truth in love" (Eph. 4:15), we should express our convictions. The final decision on a certain matter may not be in accord with either your wishes or mine. But once a given program is adopted under what the congregation feels is the leadership of the Holy Spirit, as a part of the church fellowship we should accept it as *our* program and work to make it succeed. Let me share two examples from personal experience.

Many years ago the First Baptist Church, Oklahoma City, undertook the building of a large addition to the church plant. The estimated cost was $1,200,000. At best we figured we would have a debt of $900,000. In the early 1950s, that was a lot of money.

Billy Atkinson was a deacon and a member of the building committee. As an oil man, he had lost everything in the crash of 1929 and wound up $350,000 in debt. But he promised his creditors that, given time, he would pay it with interest. And he did. (Later he became a wealthy man again.) Another deacon who was his auditor told me that Billy had requested him to set up his books so that no creditor could prevent him from tithing.

Having been burned by overextension, he did not want it to happen to his church. Billy's counsel to the building committee was to build, but to reduce the size of the project so there would be less debt. The committee voted to recommend the program as originally planned. The same thing happened when the program was presented to the deacons for study. Later the church congregation voted to adopt the recommended program.

The following Sunday morning Billy came to my study. He said, "Pastor, as you know, I did not want so large a program and debt. But the church adopted it. Never before in my life have I asked anyone to give me a job in the church. But I want you to give me a job." I said, "If I can, I will. What do you have in mind?" He said, "I want you to make me chairman of the committee to raise the money to pay that debt."

I did. And no one worked as hard as he did to make the effort succeed! We paid off the debt three years in advance. And Billy gave one-tenth of the total cost of the building.

Years later, shortly before my retirement as pastor, we were renovating the remainder of our church plant at a cost of $750,000. Mrs. Windsor was over one hundred years old. In her younger years, she had been very active in the church. Even in her nineties, she was regular in attendance. Eventually, though, she entered a nursing home, and everytime anyone from our church visited her she would send in her offering.

One day a deacon came to my study. In his hand he held a one dollar bill. With tears in his eyes he told me that when he had visited Mrs. Windsor that day, she said, "I see by the church paper that we are fixing up our buildings. I will never get to see them again, but I want to have a part in it." And she handed him that dollar bill.

The deacon said, "Preacher, this is sacred money. It is truly the 'widow's mite.' I'm turning in one of my dollars in its place. And I want to have this one framed along with its story and hang it in the Fountain Room." The Fountain Room is the large room that connects all of the buildings and is the gathering place for people after services. There it hangs today telling its beautiful story. None of us can claim to have given the "widow's mite" until we have given all we have, even our living (Luke 21:1-4).

MIssion of the Church

The mission of the church is missions. Call it evangelism, if you will. God's ancient covenant with Israel was a missionary covenant (Exod. 19:5-6). The new covenant in Christ is also a missionary covenant (1 Pet. 2:1-10), and every believer is a priest charged with carrying out that covenant.

In an earlier discussion of Matthew 16:19 we noted that Christ made his people stewards of the gospel. To take that a step further, I would say now that every believer-priest is to echo

Paul's words, "Woe is unto me, if I preach not the gospel" (1 Cor. 9:16).

Missions is the lifeblood of the churches. Due to the influence of the Judaizers (Acts 15:1, 5) the church in Jerusalem never became involved in Gentiles or foreign missions. So the center of power shifted elsewhere, in this case north to Antioch and beyond. This trend has continued through the centuries. The words of Exodus are still true: "If ye will obey my voice . . . and keep my covenant, then ye shall be a peculiar treasure. . . . And ye shall be unto me a kingdom of priests" (19:5–6). Any church or group of churches that fails to fulfill the covenant of sharing the gospel with people everywhere cannot claim the privileges and blessings of that gospel. Many years ago I often heard Dr. George W. Truett, gifted pastor of the First Baptist Church in Dallas, "Any church that is not missionary does not deserve the ground upon which its building stands." Then he would quote Psalm 24:1. "The earth is the Lord's, and the fullness thereof; the world, and they that dwell therein."

In writing to the Christians in Thessalonica, Paul praises their missionary spirit: "For from you sounded out the word of the Lord not only in Macedonia and Achaia [Greece], but also in every place your faith to God-ward is spread abroad, so that we need not to speak any thing" (1 Thess. 1:8). The words "sounded forth" are a translation of a form of the Greek verb *execheō*, a root of our word "echo." In other words the good news of the gospel "echoed out" to the entire region of Macedonia and Greece. This verb is also used for "to sound a trumpet," "to thunder," "to reverberate." "It is not amiss to liken this sounding forth to a modern broadcasting station."[3] Dr. J. B. Phillips translates it, "You have become a sort of sounding-board from which the word of the Lord has rung out."[4]

When writing to the Christians in Corinth, Paul tells how the churches of Macedonia, including Thessalonica, had out of deep poverty responded so generously to his appeal for a relief offering on behalf of Jerusalem Christians (2

Cor. 8:1–5). This was "missions in reverse." At times pastors of small churches have said to me, "I am the pastor of a little church." But then I remind them gently, "No church is *little* unless it chooses to be." Some of the greatest churches are made up of just a few people. It isn't the size that determines greatness; it is the commitment and spirit of each individual Christian or priest of God.

Over a half-century ago I read a story that compared a church to a pipe organ. A pipe organ is composed of hundreds of pipes. Some are several feet tall; others are only inches in height. Some pipes peep like birds; others rumble like thunder. They give forth their tones when the organist presses each key, causing air to rush through them. It is the combination of tones that makes beautiful music.

But just suppose a little pipe says, "I am so small compared to the large pipes. No one every hears me, because I am drowned out by the larger ones. I don't amount to anything. So when the organist presses my key I will not give off my sound." The audience hears the music and is thrilled by its beauty. But the organist, whose ears are trained to detect every sound, says, "The little pipe didn't play." This is a homely little story, but through it we are reminded that each of us is a pipe in the giant pipe organ of God. Some are large in size; others are small. But to produce spiritual music, each pipe must sound when Christ, the Master Organist, presses the key to allow the Holy Spirit, the Wind of God, to pass through its pipe.

When all of the Lord's people, great and small, sound in response to the Master's hand and in the power of the Wind of God, the result is a symphony of service that gladdens the heart of God. No matter what we may think of ourselves, each of us is important in God's purpose. So let your pipe play!

Church Polity

The priesthood of the believer is reflected in the polity of New Testament churches. For instance, Paul says that each believer's body is a temple of the Holy Spirit. The Greek word for temple is *naos*. In pagan temples, the *naos* was the place where the image of the deity was located. In the Jewish temple in Jerusalem *naos* was descriptive of the Holy of Holies where God dwelt in mercy with his people.

In 63 B.C. when the Roman general Pompey conquered Jerusalem, he "entered the Temple, and, amidst the horror of the Jews, explored the total darkness of the Holy of Holies, and found, to his great amazement, neither symbols, nor statues, nor representation of any deity."[5] This was in the Herodian Temple. When Nebuchadnezzar destroyed Solomon's Temple in 587 B.C., he took all sacred vessels to Babylon. But there was never any image that represented God in either the tabernacle or the Temple. God's presence was spiritual. In this same way, God is present in the *naos* of Christians' bodies in his Holy Spirit.

Paul echoed this idea when he told the Corinthian Christians that the church (Christians) is "the temple [*naos*] of God . . . the Spirit of God dwelleth in you" (1 Cor. 3:16). Just as the Spirit indwells each believer, so also the Spirit indwells the fellowship of a congregation of believers.

The only time in the New Testament where the Holy Spirit is seen as baptizing anyone is in 1 Cor. 12:13: "For by one Spirit are we all baptized into one body, whether we be Jews or Gentiles, whether we be bond or free; and have been all made to drink into one Spirit."

Note that Paul said "all," not merely a select group, have been baptized by the Spirit. "Baptize" may also mean to be overwhelmed (Mark 10:38–39); in this case the reference is to Jesus' atoning death. In 1 Corinthians, the reference seems to be to the Spirit indwelling the believer at the moment of regeneration (Acts 8:15; 10:44; 19:6). When we become believers in Jesus Christ, the Spirit overwhelms us as we are blended into the fellowship of believers.

Furthermore, the priesthood of the believer is reflected in the New Testament emphasis upon the local church. We have already noted that each church fellowship was a separate entity. To speak of denominations in the first century is an anachronism. However, there were forces at work in the first century that later produced the various divisions of Christianity.

The inner workings of local churches also reflect the priesthood of the believer. We see this in the congregational form of church government. It is true that the two offices in the early church were pastors and deacons. But the New Testament does not negate the creation of other positions as the need demands (for example, teachers and other leaders). But at the human level the seat of authority is the congregation.

One thing is very clear, though. When the apostles needed some men to assist them, the apostles did not choose them. Instead they said, "Wherefore, brethren, look ye out among you seven men of honest report, full of the Holy Ghost [Spirit] and wisdom, whom we may appoint over this business" (Act 6:3). The word "holy" is not in the best Greek texts, but the meaning is there. The Williams translation reads "full of the Spirit and of good practical sense."⁷ The important thing is that the congregation selected the men. And the apostles assigned them to their task.

A comparable situation is apparent when Paul urges the church at Corinth to finish taking a relief offering for the poor among the Jerusalem Christians (cf. 2 Corinthians 8-9). Each church in Macedonia and Greece, acting voluntarily, had agreed to participate, and the church at Corinth had agreed a year previously to participate (2 Cor. 8:10-24). But up to the time Paul wrote his first letter to the Corinthians, this church had not taken its offering. Now Paul, on the basis of the generous response of the Macedonian churches, exhorts them to do as they had promised (cf. 2 Cor. 8:1-6): "And when I come, whomsoever ye shall approve by your letters, them will

I send to bring your liberality [grace gift] unto Jerusalem" (1 Cor. 16:3).

The Judaizers had accused Paul of preaching for money. So, to counteract their false charges, Paul requests each church to select trustworthy people to accompany him and the offerings to Jerusalem (cf. 2 Cor. 8:19–20). The gift of relief money from each church would be carried by its personal representatives. The point being made here is that each local church on its own initiative was to take action independently.

The significant thing for us about Paul's appeal for relief money from the local churches in Macedonia and Greece was first, he as an apostle and leader did not *demand* a gift, but pleaded for one; second, no specific amount of money was levied against a particular church: each church, even each person, gave voluntarily; third, Paul did not select the people who would be in charge of the money—each local church did it for itself; fourth, from start to finish the local churches responded voluntarily.

One final example of Paul's attitude toward local church autonomy is seen in his communication with the Christians at Corinth (1 Cor. 5:1–7). While the apostle was in Ephesus, he received reports on certain problems that plagued the Corinthian church. One had to do with a member who was involved sexually with "his father's wife," evidently his stepmother.

Obviously, this gross defiance and sin demanded disciplinary action on the part of the church, but apparently the congregation was not only lax in condemning this immorality, they were "puffed up" with pride over their broad-minded attitude (1 Cor. 5:2). Knowing that something needed to be done, Paul sent the Corinthian Christians instructions: "In the name of our Lord Jesus Christ, *when ye are gathered together,* and my spirit, with the power of our Lord Jesus Christ, to deliver such an one unto Satan for the destruction of the flesh, that the spirit may be saved in the day of the Lord Jesus" (1 Cor. 5:4–5, italics mine).

This means that something is done to a person by someone else. The phrase "when ye are gathered together" translates a passive participle in the Greek original. This tells us that the congregation was brought together by someone else, perhaps the pastor or moderator. Paul then tells them that he will be with them in spirit, but they were to act under the power of the Lord Jesus. They were to take positive action against their sinning brother, but the purpose of their action is to be redemptive, not destructive. Their action was, first, to shock the man into the realization of the enormity of his sin, and then to produce repentance so that he would be forgiven before the final judgment of the Lord.

In Paul's second letter to the Corinthians, he urges the people of the church to forgive one of their members and receive him back into the church fellowship (2:5–11). I believe it is very possible that the apostle is referring to this same incident. But the point here is that the actions were to be taken by that church. It is a case of a local body of baptized believers operating through democratic processes under the lordship of Jesus Christ.

The Role of the Pastor

At this point in our discussion, it will be helpful to examine the role of the pastor in the local church. It is vitally important for us to arrive at an understanding of this in relation to the principle of the priesthood of the believer.

The writer of Hebrews states, "Obey them that have the rule over you, and submit yourselves: for they watch for your souls, as they must give account, that they may do it with joy, and not with grief: for that is unprofitable for you" (13:17). This seems to cast the pastor in the role of a ruler.

Unfortunately the King James Version translates the words "them that have the rule over you" from a Greek phrase that actually reads, "the ones leading [guiding] you." In addition, the Greek word for "obey" in this verse can also be translated "follow."[7] And the word translated "submit" can be properly translated "yield"—figuratively to "give away."

All of this may seem rather complex, but the idea the writer seems to be putting across is that they were to follow their acknowledged leaders and to voluntarily yield to them. In other words, if the people in the congregation have one idea for a church program and the pastor has another and if the difference cannot be resolved, the people should give way to the pastor's idea.

The reason given is not that the pastor has a divinely bestowed authority or the only pipeline to God but because the Lord has entrusted the pastor with responsibility for the souls of the congregation. Since God will ask for an accounting from the pastor, even if the plan fails, it should be the result of the pastor's understanding of God's will, not something that was thrust upon the pastor by others. There can be no leadership without "fellowship."

Pastoral authority is a strange sound to those who fully accept the principle of the priesthood of believers. It is true the New Testament teaches that the apostles were given a special authority. After all, the infant church of the first century did not have the New Testament because it was in process of being written. So without a guideline someone had to be in position to make decisions. However, with rare exceptions, the apostles used persuasion rather than authority. Paul's letter to Philemon is a classic example of this. But there is no evidence that this apostolic authority was passed on to others.

Perhaps the best example of the role of the pastor is seen in the story about Paul's visit with the Ephesian elders when his Jerusalem-bound ship docked at Miletus, the seaport of Ephesus (Acts 20:17–28). In his instructions to them, Paul says, "Take heed therefore unto yourselves, and to all the flock, over the which the Holy Ghost [Spirit] hath made you overseers, to feed the church of God, which he hath purchased with his own blood."

Luke says these word were spoken to the "elders" (*presbuterous*), and the Holy Spirit had placed them as "overseers" (*episkopous*, bishop, cf. 1 Tim. 3:1) over God's people. Their duty was "to feed" (*poimainein*, to tend as a shepherd, to pastor) the church of God. All three of these duties refer to the position of the person call "pastor."

In the Jewish system, *presbuteros*, or "elder," denoted men who by virtue of age and experience were capable of giving wise counsel. In the Christian sense, the title apparently did not refer so much to gage as to ability. As seen in the above treatment, "elder" is synonymous with bishop and pastor. According to one authority, "The distinction between elder or presbyter and bishop, as two separate orders of ministers dates from the 2nd century."[8]

The term "episkopos" (bishop) was used for one who oversaw the work of others. The Greek word *poimainein* means to tend as a shepherd; it is a pastoral word from which comes our word "pastor," the Latin for shepherd.

According to Paul all three of these words refer to the duties of the one office we refer to or call "pastor." As I see it "elder" suggests a counselor. "Bishop" involves administration, leadership in planning and overseeing the work and workers. "Shepherd" or "pastor" means to do for the church congregation everything a shepherd did for his sheep: feed, lead, protect, and comfort. It is true that "bishop" implies a certain amount of authority, but it is not the authority of rulership but of leadership.

In his first epistle, Peter uses the verbs for "feed" or "tend as a shepherd" (*poimainō*) and "exercising oversight" (*episkopeō*).[9] But he adds that oversight should be used not "as being lords over God's heritage, but being ensamples to the flock" (1 Pet. 5:2–3).

It isn't my intention here to in any way degrade the role of the pastor. Rather, I want to set it in proper perspective. I was a pastor for forty-four years. If I had ten thousand lives to live, I would want to be a pastor in everyone of them.

I have discovered that a wise pastor will involve his people in formulating a program. In my experience some of the richest input has come from the so-called "laity." And it is certainly true that people will work harder to achieve success in a program that they helped to plan.

This study of the role of the pastor may well be closed with words of editor Presnall H. Wood: "Pastors will do well to present themselves as pastors and not as presidents of a corporation. Churches will do well to respect the pastors and follow their leadership through the Holy Spirit. Neither pastors nor churches are infallible. They need each other."[10] To properly understand this is to authentically respect the principle of the priesthood of the believer.

Church Interrelationships

Clearly the New testament presents the centrality of local churches. And it shows that local, autonomous churches can work together for the common good. Two striking examples follow.

The first cooperative endeavor involves doctrine. We have already referred to the trouble caused by Judaizers who originally came from the Jerusalem church. These were narrow Jews who were willing for Gentiles to become Christians but who wanted them to first embrace the Jewish law and be circumcised. These Judaizers were disturbing the church at Antioch. Finally, to resolve the schism, the Antioch congregation sent representatives to consult with the church leaders in Jerusalem (cf. Acts 15; Galatians 2). At stake was the whole issue of the gospel of salvation by grace through faith. The Jerusalem Conference in A.D. 49 ruled in favor of the Gentiles being Christians without submitting to the rites of Judaism. Luke quotes James as saying, "For it seemed good to the Holy Ghost and to us, to lay upon you no greater burden than those necessary things" (Acts 15:28).

The second example involves a cooperative endeavor in financial matters—the relief offering Paul received for the destitute Jerusalem Christians (1 Cor. 16:1-4; 2 Corinthians 8-9). In both instances, the local churches acted voluntarily without surrendering any of their autonomy.

This leads me to mention the Southern Baptist Convention, a mystery both to Southern Baptists and to others. There is no organic connection between any of the churches or between local churches and various segments of Southern Baptist groups: district associations, state conventions, and the Southern Baptist Convention. No action taken by any of these organizations is binding on the others. When these organizations meet, the local churches send "messengers," not "delegates."

Delegates would carry delegated authority to those meetings, but messengers have no delegated authority. Actions taken by the messengers affect directly only the group that they make up, but they are not binding on the local churches.

Yet with this very loose relationship, Southern Baptists carry on a vigorous program of missions, Christian education, and benevolences around the world. What one local church cannot do, more than thirty-seven thousand churches can do together. And not one segment surrenders the cherished doctrine the priesthood of the believer and the autonomy of every segment of Baptist life.

Many years ago I had a friend who was a pastor and a leader in another national Baptist convention. One day he said, "Our Convention meets, adopts programs, and everyone goes home and forgets them. Southern Baptists meet, adopt programs, and everyone goes home and works to make them succeed. What kind of pressure do you use to get such cooperation?" I replied, "In all my years as a pastor, neither my church nor I have felt the pressure of one little finger. The only pressure we feel is our obligation to cooperate with our brethren in doing the Lord's work."

Baptists are not a creedal people. But through the years many Baptist bodies have drawn up *confessions of faith* or an orderly statement of faith held by a given body.[11] During the theologically turbulent 1920s, the Southern Baptist Convention adopted *The Baptist Faith and Message* (1925). In 1963 the same Convention adopted a revised edition of that statement. In order to get as close as possible to the "grass roots," the committee was composed of the presidents of the various state conventions. As president of the Southern Baptist Convention, I served as chairman.

In setting up this committee, the Convention voted that the resultant statement "*shall* serve as information to the churches, and . . . *may* serve as guidelines to the various agencies of the Southern Baptist Convention" (my italics). The preamble to this statement protects the individual conscience and guards against a creedal faith.

Various efforts to make it binding upon various church agencies have been defeated by the Convention. Yet every agency has voluntarily adopted it as its statement of faith. State conventions, district associations, and local churches have done the same thing. I know of no unit in Southern Baptist life that has refused to accept this statement. Here is a marvelous example of voluntary cooperation within the priesthood of the believer.[12]

Denominations can cooperate as long as each recognizes and respects the beliefs and practices of the others. But even in ecumenical organizations, each denomination retains its own individuality and pursues its own program.

When Jesus prayed "that they may be one, as we are" (John 17:11), he was not thinking about one apostle as large as eleven men. The key is found in the words, "as we are." God reveals himself as three persons: Father, Son, and Spirit. Yet they are one in nature and purpose. This prayer does not call for one Super-Church. But it does speak of a called-out people who believe in Jesus Christ and are committed to his redemptive purpose. In areas of mutual social interests, the Lord's people can and should cooperate without any compromise of any segment's faith and practice.

8. The Priesthood of the Believer and Religious Liberty

The history of the struggle for religious liberty is a long and bloody one. It centers in efforts to coerce the Christian conscience concerning the believers' loyalty to Christ. As we will see, this persecution of Christians emanated from both church and state.

Jewish Persecution

Christianity was cradled in persecution. Herod the Great tried to kill Jesus at his birth. The Jewish leaders hounded him during his ministry. And it was combination of church and state that brought Jesus to his death. Soon thereafter efforts were made by the Jewish Sanhedrin to suppress preaching about Christ (Acts 3–4). But Peter and John set the tone for Christian resistance to those efforts when they said, "Whether it be right in the sight of God to hearken unto you more than unto God, judge ye. For we cannot but speak the things which we have seen and heard" (Acts 4:19–20).

Following the death of Stephen, the first Christian martyr, a more vicious and widespread persecution took place under the leadership of Saul of Tarsus (cf. Acts 7:58–8:4; 9:1–2). But when he met Jesus on the Damascus road, this persecuting, bloodthirsty Pharisee became the persecuted, blood-giving Paul the apostle.

Historian Robert A. Baker says, "The principal opponents of Christ in the New Testament were Jews. His followers during the next several centuries found their most formidable foes to be the Romans."[1] However, this statement should be qualified somewhat because of the almost unspeakable persecution of Christians and under Domitian.

Pagan Persecution

The Book of Acts relates cases of pagan persecution of Christians (14:1–20; 16:19–24). But they were usually local in nature, and the persecution described in Acts 14 was actually at the instigation of the Jews.

The first major persecution of Christians triggered by the Roman government occurred toward the close of Nero's reign (A.D. 54–68). Nero made Christians the scapegoat for his burning of Rome in order to appease an angry populace. This persecution was largely local in nature. Dr. Baker says, "The death of Paul was occasioned more by the caprice of the Emperor Nero than any policy of persecuting Christians."[2]

The second major persecution of Christians occurred during the reign of Emperor Domitian (A.D. 81–96). These terror-filled times set the mood for some of what is described in the book of Revelation. But even this was not a universal movement against Christianity as such. Rather, it was directed against people who refused to participate in emperor worship. And, naturally, this included Christians. Domitian was so obsessed with being a god that it is said he refused to accept correspondence that did not address him in terms of deity. The greatest sufferers during this period seem to have been the Christians in the Roman province of Asia, a portion of Asia Minor. Since Domitian represented the Roman Empire, refusal to worship him was interpreted as disloyalty to the Empire itself.

Dr. Baker in his superb historical work points out that after the first century the opposition to Christianity took three general forms: popular antagonism, intellectual assaults, and physical persecution.[3] During this period of time an unusual number of disasters—and other calamities—plagued the Roman world. The pagan Romans claimed that their gods, angry because of this new religion, caused these climactic events. Then, either out of ignorance or by deliberate distortion of Christian teaching and practices, antagonism toward the Christians inspired accusations of atheism (no god), cannibalism (eating of the Lord's body and drinking his blood), immorality (sensual understanding of "love"), and magic and sorcery (in the Lord's Supper and baptism).

Intellectual persecution came from pagan philosophers who attacked basic Christian beliefs: the Christian Scriptures, grace, regeneration, heaven and hell, and immortality. Principal among these were Celsus and Pophyro, Greek philosophers of the second and third centuries respectively.

In same ways, though, the intellectual persecution became a blessing in disguise, since it forced Christian apologists to hammer out logical and reasonable explanations of Christian truth. Chief among these defenders of the faith was Justin Martyr, a Samaritan philosopher who became a Christian. He was martyred in A.D. 166.

Physical persecution followed the destruction of Jerusalem in A.D. 70, when it became clear that Christianity was not merely a branch of Judaism. Judaism under the Roman system was a legal religion. Consequently, a separate movement like Christianity was considered an illegal religion.[4].

Following Domitian's death in A.D. 96, his successor Nerva (A.D. 96–98) left the Christians in peace. For the first thirteen years of his reign, Trajan (A.D. 98–117) did the same. While certain emperors during the following years were occasionally guilty of Christian persecution, it is generally accepted that Emperor Trajan closed out the old system of "uncompromising hostility."[5]

Persecution of Christians by the Roman Empire ended in March, A.D. 313, when Constantine issued the Edict of Milan granting individual freedom of religious belief.[6]

Constantine and Christianity

Having defeated all his rivals, Emperor Constantine became the sole ruler of the Roman Empire. His mother had been a Christian, and his father looked favorably upon Christianity.

Constantine shared his father's attitude, and in A.D. 311 he fought a crucial battle just outside the walls of Rome with his last remaining rival Maxentius. In a dream before this bitter battle Constantine saw a cross in the sky and the words, "In this sign conquer." It was this that convinced him of the superiority of the Christian religion. However, Constantine retained the pagan religions, even keeping the title as their chief priest. After his death in 337, paganism made him one of its deities.

We can hardly say that Constantine ever actually became a Christian. Believing that baptism washed away sins, he delayed being baptized until just before he died. Nevertheless he created the atmosphere that finally led the Emperor Theodosius (378–395) to declare Christianity the state religion of the Empire.[7]

Christians certainly must have breathed sighs of relief when Roman persecution ceased. But actually Christianity fared better under persecution than under the new order. Once it became fashionable to be a Christian, hordes of unredeemed people professed to believe, but did not really become Christians.

Actually Constantine's recognition of Christianity was more political than spiritual. He saw in the Christian movement the one power that could be a binding element in stabilizing his crumbling empire. Furthermore, his recognition of Christianity brought about a union of church and state that lasted until colonial times in America. Under this unholy union, the church lost much of its vigor as corruption entered into its life stream.

The growing power of the Christian movement led to the struggle for supremacy between the church and the state. "Between the Council of Nicea of 324 and the fourth Lateran Council of 1215 the Roman bishop [pope] had become master of the world spiritual and secular."[8] And in this almost one-thousand-year struggle, New Testament Christianity was the greatest casualty. The simple New JTestament order had been replaced by the hierarchical structure of the church, and the principle of the priesthood of the believer and religious liberty were lost.

The abuses and excesses practiced in the name of religion during this period of church and world history sparked the flames that produced the Protestant Reformation in the early years of the sixteenth century under the bold leadership of Martin Luther. But even following the Protestant Reformation, the struggle for religious liberty continued. In England there was a long struggle as to whether the Roman Catholic or Protestant faith would become the established church. Today the Presbyterian faith is the state church in Scotland and the Church of England (Anglican) is the state church in England. However, it was the religious climate in England that sparked the early struggle for religious liberty in America.[9]

Liberty and Toleration

The establishment of a state church in a country accentuates the difference between religious liberty and religious toleration. Historian Robert Baker explains this difference: "By the time Elisabeth [sic] died in 1603, England had a strong Protestant government. This did not mean, however, that dissent would be permitted, for religious dissent could not be differentiated from civil rebellion in a realm where church and state were united under one sovereign."[10]

The religious climate in England is quite different today. Wherever an established church exists, it means that many people are taxed to support a faith different from theirs. In addition, they completely finance their own religious activities and institutions. That is not liberty but toleration, and there is a vast difference between the two. For one thing, this kind of toleration denies the priesthood of the believer.

One of the greatest sermons on religious liberty was preached by Dr. George W. Truett in May 1920 from the steps of the Capitol in Washington, D.C. In it he clearly set forth the differences between religious liberty and religious toleration.

According to Dr. Truett, "Toleration implies that somebody falsely claims the right to tolerance. Toleration is a concession, while liberty is a right. Toleration is a matter of expediency while liberty is a matter of principle. Toleration is a gift from man, while liberty is a gift from God. It is the consistent and insistent contention of our Baptist people, always and everywhere, that religion must be forever voluntary and uncoerced. And that it is not the prerogative of any power, whether civil or ecclesiastical, to compel man to conform to any religious creed or form of worship, or to pay taxes for the support of a religious organization to which they do not belong and in whose creed they do not believe. God wants free worshipers and no other kind."[12]

Dr. Truett then added, "Years ago, at a notable dinner in London, that world-famed statesman, John Bright, asked an American statesman, himself a Baptist, the noble Dr. J. L. M. Curry, 'What distinct contribution has your America made to the science of government?' To that question Dr. Curry replied, 'The doctrine of religious liberty.' Mr. Bright made the worthy reply, 'It was a tremendous contribution.' "[12]

The Struggle for Religious Liberty in America

In chapter 2 I referred to the struggle in America for religious liberty and the part Baptists played in it. At the heart of this struggle was the relationship between church and state. This grew out of the unhappy experience of dissenters in Europe, especially England, over the establishment of one state church and the resultant hardships placed upon all others.

The ideal, however, is "A Free Church in a Free State."[13] This ideal has become more nearly a reality in the United States than anywhere else in the world. But it was "a pearl of great price." And the price was great suffering on the part of those who fought for it.

"Those who fought so vigorously for religious liberty in America were a special breed of people. A strong democratic spirit and the principle of separation of church and state greatly influenced, and gave direction to the religious life of the United States."[14] However, not all shared this feeling. Principal among them were the Congregationalists in Massachusetts and the Church of England in Virginia. Both colonies had state churches.[15]

For instance, "In 1631 the [Massachusetts] colony enacted a regulation that only the members of the Congregational churches could be free men. Thus the ministers of the local congregations were able to regulate suffrage on the basis of religious orthodoxy. ... The Massachusetts Bay Colony was completely intolerant of Separatism" or anyone outside their group. Thus when Roger Williams, a Baptist, arrived in 1631 and denounced their system, efforts were made to silence him. In 1636 he was banished in the dead of winter. He would have died were it not for the aid of friendly Indians. In 1638 he founded Providence Plantation, which later became the colony of Rhode Island. The following year he organized what was perhaps the first Baptist church in America.[16]

The colony of Rhode Island guaranteed religious liberty and the separation of church and state. This was the first government since Constantine to do so.

According to Dr. Robert Baker, "the victory for religious liberty began in Virginia.[17] The Baptists, led by the preacher John Leland, were strongly aided by the Presbyterians and Methodists, together with the political help of James Madison. They succeeded in blocking at the federal level the establishment of a state religion in 1787. Virginia ratified the federal Constitution with the understanding that, immediately upon its adoption by the Constitutional Convention, a bill of rights that guaranteed religious liberty would be added. This finally led to the adoption of the First Amendment to the United States Constitution.

Dr. Frank Mead, a leading Methodist writer, gives two thrilling accounts from the struggle in Virginia. One of the stories is about three Baptist preachers: John Waller, Louis Craig, and James Childs. They were arrested for preaching contrary to the established church. In court, a wild-eyed prosecuting attorney cried above the hubbub, "May it please your worship, these men are great disturbers of the peace; they cannot meet a man upon the road, but they must ram a text of scripture down his throat."

It looked bad for the defendants. Fifty miles away a young Scottish-American lawyer named Patrick Henry (a good Episcopalian) heard of it, turned red to the roots of his hair, saddled his horse and galloped into town. Waving the indictment above his head in a fury wilder than that of the prosecuting attorney, he roared, "For preaching the gospel of God. Great God! Great God!! Great God!!!"[18]

The preachers were acquitted.

The other account involves John Leland and James Madison. Following the Revolutionary War, the federal Constitution was drawn up, but it had to be ratified by the colonies. The colonies were dubious of any centralized authority. But one by one they voted to ratify the document

"Finally, Massachusetts and Virginia became the pivotal states in the fight. They must pass it, or the whole thing would be lost. Massachusetts fell into line with an early election and that left Virginia. Now Madison was running for the state legislature of Virginia against Baptist elder, John Leland, of Orange County. Madison's presence in that body was necessary to ratify the Constitution, and Madison was beaten before the election! Orange was overwhelmingly Baptist. Madison hadn't a chance. Leland knew that. He also knew that without Madison's golden voice and political influence, there would be no Constitution. So, with victory already in his hand, he dropped out of the race and gave Madison an open road. The rest is history.[19]

Another story concerning the quest for religious liberty in Virginia came to me from the late L. L. Gwaltney, a Virginian and a well-known editor. As a child his grandfather had accompanied his father to the funeral of a Virginia Baptist preacher. When they viewed the body of the dead preacher, they noticed that his hands were full of scars. When the boy asked about the scars, his father told him this story:

In colonial days in Virginia the preacher was arrested for preaching the gospel contrary to the teaching of the state church. HIs people would gather outside his jail cell to hear him preach, but the authorities had a high fence built so the people couldn't see him. They came anyway, so he continued to preach to them.

While he was preaching, he would extend his arms between the bars. The guards on duty would then slash at his hands with sharp knives, leaving deep scars.[20] What a price that pioneer preacher paid for his convictions on the priesthood of the believer.

The First Amendment and Its Meaning

The Declaration of Independence is one of the greatest documents ever written. Yet, strangely it does not mention religious persecution among its grievances. And as I've already mentioned, neither did the Constitution itself. It remained for the First Amendment to provide a guarantee of religious liberty. The first line of this amendment reads, "Congress shall make no law respecting the establishment of religion, or prohibiting the free exercise thereof." We cannot fail to see in these few words a bastion of security for the priesthood of the believer from governmental interference.

What does this portion of the First Amendment really mean? First, it clearly forbids the official establishment of a state church in the United States.

Furthermore, the First Amendment forbids laws that prohibit the free exercise of any and all religions. Neither can the state coerce its citizens to be religious or to recognize any deity. This is a matter between the individual person and God. It does not forbid the use of "In God We Trust" and "under God" on our coins or in the Pledge of Allegiance to the flag respectively, since it does not specify any one deity by name. This is because the vast majority of our citizens believe in a Supreme Being.

The First Amendment does recognize the competency of the soul in religion, the priesthood of the believer, the right of direct access to God, and the freedom of choice with respect to religion. This is religious freedom, not toleration.

Clearly the First Amendment prohibits the use of church money for governmental purposes and the use of governmental money for religious purposes. To paraphrase Kipling, tithes are tithes and taxes are taxes, and never the twain shall meet. We know from sad experience that what government finances, it ultimately will control.

This amendment recognizes that the church has no civic function, and the state has no ecclesiastical function. Neither should attempt to control the other. The state should not try to tell the church how to do its work; the church should not try to tell the state how to run its business. The First Amendment was born out of the European background where the state and the church tried to control each other; it is a protest against both.

As Christian citizens, we should exert our influence in the interest of good government. The New Testament repeatedly teaches that Christians should be good citizens. But no corporate segment of Christianity should deliver a mandate to any area of civil government. The First Amendment gives the right "to petition the Government for a redress of grievances," but that is miles away from being a mandate.

Admittedly there are gray areas in the relationship between church and state. Even the best constitutional lawyers have difficulty in interpreting them, but again certain things are clear. For example, there is the matter of parochial and private schools. Certainly the state has no right to forbid them, but it does have the right to set academic standards if their graduates are to be admitted to public schools of higher learning.

Perhaps no decision by the United States Supreme Court has caused more confusion than the one on prayer in public schools. Unfortunately, the initial report stated that the Court had outlawed prayer in public schools. But did it? Actually, the issue was not voluntary prayer as such. Instead, it was whether or not an agency or agent of government could compose a prayer and require that it be used. The Court correctly ruled that this violated the First Amendment. To have ruled otherwise would have blurred the boundaries between church and state. But voluntary prayer was never the issue.

However, the fact remains that the Bible places the responsibilities for Bible study and prayer in the home and church. And that is where the priesthood of the believer enters the picture.

Relations Between Church and State

The First Amendment is not a wall blocking the mutual relationship of church and state. The state is to provide a climate in which the church can do its work. The church is to produce Christian citizens who make for good government. There are areas in which church and state can help each other. Even little things like a church permitting the use of space in its building for voter registration and voting, or allowing the government to use space for storing emergency food and equipment in case of a disaster. But, of course, the government should never attempt to commandeer church buildings, or property for any purpose. There are times of emergency, however, when our needs cannot be met by either church or state alone. This calls for cooperative effort.

During World War II, I was pastor of a church in Alexandria, Louisiana, the most concentrated troop-training area in the nation. Thousands of men were in three Army camps and several airfields. Many servicemen's wives came to be near their husbands as long as possible. Soon Alexandria became the "baby boom" capital of the nation. Military hospitals were not equipped to meet the need, and our Baptist hospital's facilities were inadequate for so large demand. At the time, I happened to be chairman of the operating committee of the hospital.

The commanding general of the area came to me with the request (not a command) that we erect an obstetrics building on land we owned adjacent to the hospital. I told him that while we had the land, we didn't have the money. He said that the military would not even be able to staff a hospital if they built it, but they could furnish the money if we would build and staff it.

I presented the matter to our committee. Immediately we faced the church-state problem. Nevertheless, all of the committee members except one were ready to proceed with the project. The objector said, "I do not believe in accepting anything from the government without paying for it." I asked, "If your church building were on fire, would you call the fire department?" "Of course!" he said. "Would you expect to pay for it?" "Of course not!" And to that I replied, "Then you would be accepting service provided by tax funds." He said, "Well, I guess our house is on fire." So we agreed to do it.

We were faced with a dire human emergency. Like the Pharisees we might have valued our institution more than meeting human need. But we could not see Jesus' doing that. We, along with the general, wanted to meet the need. We each had something the other could not supply, so we came together as equals. In drawing up the agreement, the government's lawyer was as careful as we were not to violate the First Amendment. Proper safeguards were taken at each step of the way. We received no gift from the state. The state received no gift from the church. But state and church worked together as partners in mercy to meet human need. We remained a free church in a free state.

Lessons about Liberty

Volumes could be written on this subject, but all I've attempted here is to give a brief sketch of the struggle for religious liberty. Our ancestors paid a high price to give us the freedom we enjoy, a freedom that we must not lose or scorn. Benjamin Franklin once said, "They that give up essential liberty to obtain temporary safety deserve neither liberty nor safety." And Edmund Burke reminds us that "people never give up their liberties but under some delusion."

There aren't shortcuts on the road to freedom. Satan offered Jesus a shortcut that would presumably attract converts but avoid the high price of the cross. But Jesus refused. Indeed eternal vigilance is the price of freedom.

Truly religious liberty is the mother of all liberties. And at the heart of religious liberty is the priesthood of the believer. It involves the right of direct access to God, but it also entails the responsibility of leading others to him.

In the religious freedom that is ours in Christ, we need to commit both to memory and to life the words the Apostle Paul wrote to the Christians at Corinth, "Therefore if any man be in Christ, he is a new creature [creation], old things are passed away: behold all things are become new. And all things are of God, who hath reconciled us to himself by Jesus Christ, and hath given to us the ministry of reconciliation; To wit, that God was in Christ, reconciling the world unto himself . . . and hath committed unto us the word of reconciliation. Now then we are ambassadors for Christ, as though God did beseech you by us we pray you in Christ's stead [as his substitute, on his behalf], be ye reconciled to God" (2 Cor. 5:19–20).

Freedom in Christ is not merely something to be enjoyed. It is something to be shared.

9. The Priesthood of the Believer and You

Several years ago, Dr. Andrew W. Blackwood delivered a series of lectures on preaching at Southwestern Baptist Theological Seminary in Ft. Worth, Texas. One evening after a lecture a group gathered in a home for refreshments, fellowship, and to "pick the preacher's brain." Someone asked Dr. Blackwood, "What one suggestion would you make as to how to improve preaching?" He replied, "Say 'you,' not 'we.' " It is an excellent suggestion.

Everyone in the audience can hide behind "we" or else get lost behind the crowd. The most preached-to person in a congregation is "Um." "The preacher sure did hit 'Um,' didn't he?" But when you say "you," every serious listener will feel that the speaker is talking to him or her.

Jesus applied this method near Caesarea Philippi when he asked, "Whom do men say that I the Son of man am?" The apostles replied by naming the varied opinions floating about Galilee. Then Jesus asked, "But whom say ye that I am?" (Matt. 16:13–16). "Ye" is emphatic. "But *you*, whom do *you* say that I am?" It made little difference as to the varied opinions held by the crowd as to Jesus' identity. But for those who took the matter seriously and on whose shoulders rested the responsibility for carrying on Jesus' work, the matter was of supreme importance. If they had the proper concept of Jesus and his mission, the work would go forward.

The same is true of you as a priest of God. So far I have presented the concept of the priesthood of the believer in principle and have tried to show how the various tides of history have affected it. Despite the efforts of some to destroy or deny this concept, it has endured. But now is future and effectiveness come down to *you*. Yes, and to *me*. How will this precious doctrine fare through us? For even though battles have been won, the war is not over.

Race Before Us

Hebrews 11 may well be called the "Westminster Abbey of the Bible." Westminster Abbey in London is the burial place of many of England's great. The most prominent place in the Abbey, right in front of the altar, is the burial place of David Livingstone, the missionary to Africa. It suggests that despite kings, queens, and conquerors, the greatest contribution of an empire is symbolized by a lonely missionary. Indeed, the final issues in life are spiritual.

This marvelous "faith chapter" contains the roll call of the heroes and heroines of faith. Each in his or her own time and way faithfully filled a role assigned by God.

As I mentioned earlier, the overall picture in this roll call of faith is that of a relay race. A relay team is composed of several runners, with each running a segment of the race before passing the baton on to the next runner. A team has not won the race until the last member crosses the finish line.

The list of team members in Hebrews 11 is so long that the author finally stops naming them and instead mentions their actions. He then closes with this significant statement, "And these all, having obtained a good report [witnessing] through faith, received not the promise [final victory]; God having provided some better thing for us, that they without us should not be made perfect [reach the final goal]" (Heb. 11:39–40).

The point is that each one of the people mentioned throughout the chapter has successfully completed his or her segment of the race. But the overall victory depends on everyone, including us, who follow after them.

Up to now in our discussion, our emphasis has focused on the price paid by our ancestors in the faith that they might pass on to us the torch of religious freedom, a vital part of which is the doctrine of the priesthood of the believer. But the race is not finished. It must go on until he who places us in its says, "It is enough."

We do not know when the race will be finished. That moment is hidden in the mind of the Father (Acts 1:7). You might ask, "Is my segment the last to be run?" Actually, that is not your concern. Your only concern is to run successfully your part of the race. If the Lord delays his return a thousand years or more, the record will still show what you did in your time. So your sole responsibility is to run well. In order to do that, each one of us must be attentive to certain things.

Privilege and Responsibility

The privilege of religious freedom is not something that can be taken for granted. You are free because God created you as a person capable of having direct access to him. This means no institution or person can come between you and God. You need no mediator other than Christ Jesus in prayer, confession, forgiveness, and fellowship with God. Through the Holy Spirit, you can read and interpret God's word for yourself. You enjoy absolute freedom in your relationship with God. And you enjoy these privileges because others before you were faithful in their part of the race.

Freedom in religion does not mean freedom *from* religion. Freedom of worship does not mean freedom *from* worship. You have the right of private worship, indeed, it is necessary for a well-rounded Christian life. But also you are urged not to neglect coming together with others in corporate worship (Heb. 10:25).

Since my wife went to be with the Lord, I eat alone much of the time. But something is missing; it is table fellowship. At times I go to the grocery store when I don't really need anything except to be with people. This is also true in worship. Yes, we need quiet time alone with God. But God made us as gregarious beings. "It is not good that the man should be alone" is true spiritually as well as socially. "Loners" are the exception and not the rule in life.

This thought bridges over from privilege to responsibility. For while you need to worship with others, in doing so you influence others. As a priest, you are responsible for influencing people who aren't Christian to a saving faith in Jesus Christ. Furthermore, you—and I—are to live the kind of life that strengthens and encourages other believers.

Not only should you avail yourself of the privilege of priesthood, but you are to shoulder the responsibilities of the priesthood. The tragic mistake of the people of Israel was to remember the "then" and to forget the "if" that the writer of Exodus spoke about (19:5-6). To use a Christian term, the Israelites were to evangelize pagan nations, not be paganized by them. Unfortunately, it didn't turn out that way, and they lost their opportunity in God's redemptive purpose.

The writer of Hebrews spoke of "the sin which does so easily beset us" (12:1). He was referring here, I believe, to the fact that as citizens of this world, we wrestle with the dilemma of our identity. And in dealing with this problem, we confront two extremes, both of which are wrong. You can become a recluse from the world, spending your time and energy in the saving of your own soul. Or you can become a part of the world's evil system. Neither will lead a lost world to Christ.

The Lord's instructions are clear. You are to be *in* the world, but not become a part of its system. In the New Testament, the word "world" is used in the spiritual sense of a world system that takes no thought of God. In such a system Jesus said, "Ye are the salt of the earth. ... [Y]e are the light of the world" (Matt. 5:13-14). Salt not only gives zest, it preserves. But for salt to do its work it must come into contact with its object. In doing so, though, it still remains salt.

The Lord made it clear, too, that a light is not to be hidden. It is to shine. In fact, if you are really lighted, you *will* shine. And if you are to shine, you must constantly submit to God's cleansing process of forgiveness, praying for strength to overcome temptation.

The self-righteous Pharisees of Jesus' time criticized him for eating with publicans and sinners (cf. Matt. 9:11–13). If effect he replied, "Where would you expect to find a physician?" The answer was obvious: with sick people. But the physician was not to become ill himself through exposure but was to be used as an instrument of God in healing them. We have no better model for our actions than Jesus. You should take your cue from Him.

In the parable of the good Samaritan (Luke 10:25–37), Jesus was not telling the Jewish lawyer how to be saved. Instead, he was telling him how to be a good neighbor. But then the lawyer wanted to split hairs in defining "neighbor." Instead of giving him a textbook definition, Jesus painted a portrait of a good neighbor. The picture story of the good Samaritan shows him instead of telling him what the word meant.

As the story unravels, we become a part of the scene. A Jewish traveler on the Jericho road had been robbed, beaten, and left for dead. Then Jesus introduced two characters, a priest and a Levite. In the Greek text of the story, the actions of the priest and Levite are most picturesque. As each one came down the road, he saw the poor man, lying in the middle of the road. Fearful of becoming ceremonially unclean by touching him, they "passed by on the other side" (Luke 10:31–32). In Greek this means that they literally moved to the side of the road, passed by, and then moved back to the middle of the road to resume their journey. It is obvious that the two men the lawyer would have expected to be neighborly were not!

Continuing the story, Jesus said, "But a certain Samaritan . . . came where he was. . . . [H]e had compassion on him." The word "but" is used to set the Samaritan over against the priest and Levite. The Samaritan dared to get his hands dirty, or bloody, in order to minister to a helpless man. Rendering first aid, he then helped the robbery victim to a nearby inn and "took care of him" (Luke 10:34). The idea suggested in the story is that the Samaritan personally cared for the injured man through the night.

Next, we are told that the man's condition was so improved by morning that the Samaritan traveler could leave him and go on his way, but before going he gave the innkeeper money to pay for the man's care until he was well.

Why did Jesus in telling the story choose a Samaritan for the hero? It was because a Samaritan was the one person in the world most unlikely to minister to a Jew. I can't help but wonder who would be the hero if Jesus was telling that story today in your town and mine. How do we react to persons of difference races, social structures, and religious preferences? Would we stoop to touch and help such a person with an obvious need?

Someone has suggested three philosophies of life in the Parable of the good Samaritan: What is yours is mine, and I will take it (robbers). What is mine is mine, and I will keep it (priest and Levite). What is mine is yours, and I will share it (Samaritan).

To Jesus' question as to which of these "was neighbor unto him that fell among thieves?" the lawyer replied with the obvious answer. But note that he did not say "Samaritan." He would have choked on that word. Instead, he said, "He that shewed mercy on him" (Luke 10:37). And in reply Jesus said, "Go, and do thou likewise."

Jesus is saying the same to you! Yes, and to me! The world is ravaged by sin. The highways of the world are strewn with broken bodies, ruined souls, and aching spirits. And the Lord wants to minister to them through those who believe in him. But too often we merely ask, "Who is my neighbor?"

Practically speaking, who is your neighbor? "Neighbor" means "nigh-dweller." If someone calls from his yard and you hear him, he is your neighbor. If from your home you can see him, he is your neighbor. By means of electronics you can sit in your home and both hear and see those on the other side of the world. You can hear their agonizing cry for help. You can see them in the throes of darkness, hunger, and suffering. They are your neighbors—whether they live across the street or around the world. And Jesus is saying, "Go, and do thou likewise."

Debtorship

The book of Romans is the greatest of all expositions of the gospel. While in Corinth, Paul anticipated a missionary trip to Spain. On his way he planned to visit the church in Rome. This church had been founded before Paul had even set foot on Macedonian soil. While there were Christians in Rome whom he had known elsewhere (cf. Romans 16), most of the people there had never heard him preach. So anticipating this visit, he wrote a letter in which he explained the gospel as he preached it.

For our purpose now, this statement is significant: "I am debtor both to the Greeks, and to the Barbarians; both to the wise, and to the unwise. So, as much as in me is, I am ready to preach the gospel to you that are in Rome also" (Rom. 1:14–15).

Paul had preached the gospel in the hinterlands of Galatia (Acts 13–14), in the university city of Athens (Acts 17), and in the wicked city of Corinth (Acts 18). It had borne fruit wherever he had proclaimed it. He is certain the same will be true in the capital city of Rome.

However, Paul's sense of debtorship is highly significant. The Jews divided the human race into Jews and Gentiles. The Greeks divided it into Greeks and Barbarians. Barbarians were not savages; they were non-Greek speaking people. To the Greeks any language other than Greek sounded like *bar bar*. So they put them together to form the word *barbaros*, barbarian. The words "wise" and "unwise" also divide the human race into two groups. So, in effect, Paul is saying that he is in debt to the entire human race.

Paul's sense of debtorship did not rest upon what these people had done for him. For the most part all they had done was give him a rough time. Rather, he considered himself a debtor because of what God in Christ had done for him, and he was under obligation to share that good news with every person on earth. Paul took seriously the priesthood of the believer. Joyously he accepted the privileges; loyally he discharged the responsibilities.

On his desk, a pastor had a plaque that read, "The world is still waiting to see what God can do through one man who is wholly committed to his will." When I read that, my reaction was that if the world had not seen this in Paul, it never would see it. He was Christ's greatest interpreter and the greatest missionary the world has ever known. More than any other follower of Christ, under the leadership of the Holy Spirit he molded the pattern of the Christian movement. Some interpreters have suggested that the church should be called "Pauline" rather than "Christian." While I don't subscribe to that view, it does reflect the tremendous impact that this "servant" (slave, *doulos*) of Christ made upon Christianity.

This review of Paul's importance helps us better understand his request of the Christians at Philippi. "Brethren, be followers together of me" (Phil. 3:17). In Greek the idea of the words "followers together" means to mimic or imitate. One authority suggests it could read, "Keep your eyes on me as goal."[1] Also in this verse Paul refers to himself as an "example" (*tupon*), or type.

Of course, Christ is the supreme example. And for anyone other than Paul this statement would be the height of egotism. But for him it comes naturally. With all of Paul's human frailties, he was wholly committed to the will of the Lord.

Paul was always hesitant to speak of his accomplishments in the Lord's work, lest he appear to boast (2 Cor. 11:23). He did so only to answer his critics. As a matter of fact, Paul referred to his greatest spiritual experience as though it happened to someone else (2 Cor. 12:1–12). Yet he didn't hesitate to challenge his Philippian readers to pattern their Christian lives after him. As priests of Christ, we should be able to do the same thing.

The Will of God

Jesus always followed the will of his Father. He said on one occasion, "My meat is to do the will of him that sent me, and to finish his work" (John 4:34). And he did exactly that, even though it led him to the cross (Matt. 26:36-42). And in turn urged all who follow him to "deny himself, and take up his cross" (Matt. 16:24-26).

However, Jesus does not ask you to do anything that he has not already done. As your high priest, Jesus made the supreme sacrifice; indeed, he was both priest and sacrifice.

Paul's pattern in writing was, first, to explain the doctrine, and, then, to apply it. In Romans 1-11, Paul explains the gospel. Beginning with chap. 12, he applies it. He opens with these words, "I beseech ye therefore, brethren, by the mercies of God, that ye present your bodies a living sacrifice, holy, acceptable unto God, which is your reasonable service. and be not conformed to this world: but be ye transformed by the renewing of your mind, that ye may prove what is that good, and acceptable, and perfect will of God" (Rom. 12:1-2).

His use of the word "therefore" in v. 1 ties this application section to the explanation chapters. Master logician and theologian that he was, he presented the gospel in one of the greatest pieces of logic in all literature. Even though he was without parallel as a theological thinker, Paul never divorced belief from behavior. Christian faith not only should result in Christian living, but Paul, like James (see James 2), believed that one should prove faith by works.[2]

Paul's use of the Greek word translated "beseech," in this case means to encourage or exhort. In other words, Paul is exhorting them on the basis of God's mercy revealed in Christ Jesus.

Continuing our examination of Rom. 12:1, the Jewish historian Josephus wrote that the verb for "present" was used of a priest bearing the sacrifice to the Lord. So, in this case, unlike the Jewish priests in Old Testament times who offered a dead sacrifice on the altar, these "priests" are told to present living bodies at God's altar. This is an apt picture of every priest of God. And like Jesus in his redemptive work, so you in your offering are both priest and sacrifice in your service for God.

In Rom. 12:2, Paul gives us both the negative and positive sides of the Christian walk. Literally, he says, "Stop being conformed to this age." The word "conformed" means to be fashioned according to another's pattern. This suggests appearing on the outside to be what you are not on the inside. Since Paul is writing to Christians, he tells them they should stop giving the outward appearance of being worldly. The passive voice of the Greek verb means that the mores of the age are fashioning a person's outward conduct contrary to his or her Christian profession.

On the other hand, the Greek word translated "transformed" means to appear on the outside what you are on the inside. Again the passive voice means that you are being transformed by someone else—the Holy Spirit.[3]

In chapter 4 we noted the threefold nature of salvation: regeneration, sanctification, and glorification. Regeneration, or the saving of the soul, came through repentance from sin and faith in Jesus Christ. As a believer, you became a priest of God. Simultaneously you were sanctified, or set apart, as God's vessel for his use. This involves the saving of your Christian life as you develop and serve the Lord. It is as a sanctified believer that you are to serve as a priest of God. The Holy Spirit is active in both these phases of full redemption. In and through the transforming power of the Holy Spirit, you are being made into the likeness of Jesus Christ so that others will see Jesus in you.

Your life's a book before their eyes, They're reading it through and through; Say, does it point them to the skies, Do others see Jesus in you?[4]

The goal of the process Paul speaks of (Rom. 12:2) is expressed by the Greek preposition *eis*, which means "unto" or "looking toward," followed by the present infinitive of the Greek word *dokimazein*, "to prove by testing." Literally, the last part of v. 2 reads, "looking toward repeated proof by testing with respect to oneself what God's will is—the good, and acceptable [well pleasing] and perfect [complete]" will. In other words, we are to test God's will and as we do, we will find it meets all the specifications for our Christian life and we then place our approval on it.[5]

Dr. George W. Truett, one of the greatest Christians I ever knew, was fond of saying, "To know the will of God is the greatest knowledge. To do the will of God is the greatest achievement. The will of God is not always easy, but it is always right." At Dr. Truett's funeral, an open New Testament was placed in his left hand, with the index finger of his right hand pointing to "Thy will be done" (Matt 6:10). It was the guiding star of his life. May it be yours and mine as well.

Centers of Concern

There are three centers of concern for each of us as we live out our priesthood of believers role. They are (1) leading lost people to a saving experience with Jesus Christ; (2) developing Christian character into the likeness of Jesus Christ; and (3) ministering to the needy, whoever and wherever they might be.

Conversion to a Christian experience is more than reformation; it is regeneration. The story is told about a Communist on a soapbox who pointed to a shabbily dressed man and said, "Communism will put a new suit on that man." A Christian in the crowd said, "Christ will put a new man in that suit." This illuminates the difference between what is sometimes called a purely "social gospel" and the gospel of Christ.

I said earlier, the Christian message is a spiritual gospel that has social implications—and in that order. A good example of this is found in the Gospel of Mark (2:3–12). In this story, Jesus first forgave the paralyzed man's sins (v. 5). Then Jesus healed his body (vv. 9–12). Even where this order was not followed, as in the case of the man born blind (John 9:1–37), the healing was done (v. 7) in order to lead him to a saving faith in Jesus (vv. 35–38). Social ministries are a means to an end, and not the end itself.

Nicodemus was a distinguished Pharisee and "a ruler of the Jews." Yet Jesus said, "Ye must be born again [from above]" (John 3:7). The new birth is not an option; it is a necessity. The word "must" in v. 7 is a translation of a Greek word that expresses a moral and spiritual necessity. Through his natural birth, Nicodemus was born into an earthly family with earthly relationships. But through the birth from above, he would be born into a spiritual family with spiritual relationships. And if that didn't happen, he would not be able to "see the kingdom of God" (John 3:3).

Throughout the Gospels, we see that Jesus was frequently a guest in people's homes. But we only know of one time when he asked to be a guest: "Zacchaeus, make haste, and come down; for today I must abide at thy house" (Luke 19:5).

Apparently Zacchaeus was one of the most despised men in Jericho. Publicans, or tax-collectors, were generally hated. Since they collected Roman taxes, they were regarded as traitors to their own country and relegated to the bottom of the social ladder.

Under the Roman system, the right to collect taxes in a given area went to the highest bidder. In collecting taxes, Zacchaeus had the power of the Roman army behind him. Jericho was a choice "plum" in this system. And since Zacchaeus was the "chief," evidently he had received the right to collect taxes in that area.

It was Zacchaeus's job to collect enough tax money to meet his assessment, plus a fat profit for himself. This system invited corruption and extortion. There was no doubt about it, Zacchaeus did his dirty job well—he was rich.

According to the story, when the people of Jericho saw Jesus enter his home, they were outraged and accused Jesus of being a "guest with a man that is a sinner" (Luke 19:7). The word "murmured" in v. 7 translates the Greek word, *diegogguzon*, which when pronounced sounds like the buzzing of angry bees.

If Jesus had marched at the head of a picket line carrying a sign, demanding that Zacchaeus mend his way, he would have been acclaimed a hero by the people. But that would only have made Zacchaeus mad. Instead Jesus entered his home and led him to a personal faith in God. The proof of this transformation is found in Zacchaeus's own words, "Lord, the half of my goods I give to the poor; and if I have taken anything from any man by false accusation, I restore him fourfold" (Luke 19:8). Zacchaeus was no longer a crooked tax collector but a Christian tax commissioner! That's the way Jesus did things and he is our model.

In both the natural and the spiritual world, being born is only the beginning. In either case, we dare not leave the newborn babe to fend for itself. Birth implies a continuing process. In the spiritual sense, it means saving the Christian life.

Considering the need and the relatively small number of Christians who take seriously the responsibilities of the priesthood of the believer, our record in birthing children into the family of God and nourishing them is not something we can be proud of. Our record of nourishing and growing strong and productive adult Christians is shameful.

In 1954 I was asked to write a small book on Hebrews to be used by Southern Baptists as the 1955 January Bible study book. In it I warned Christians about losing their opportunity to be used by God in his redemptive purpose. The man who was to edit the manuscript through publication had another view. He said, "My wife and I are Christians. Our son is a Christian. And we have a Christian home. That is about all we can do."

I told him that is exactly the attitude against which the book of Hebrews warns us. We are to avoid that kind of sterile inbreeding. We are not merely to look after "our own," but we are to be witnessing evangelists in a pagan world.

At the same time, our evangelist ministry is to help the unfortunate all about us. The spiritual gospel has powerful social implications. The writer of James drives this point home when he says, "What doth is profit, my brethren, though a man say he hath faith, and have not works? Can faith save him?" (2:14) Literally this means "Can that kind of faith save him?" A saving faith is a working faith. Paul makes the same point when he says this to the Christians in Ephesus, "For we are his [God's] workmanship, created in Christ Jesus *unto good works*, which God hath before ordained that we]should walk in them" (Eph. 2:10, italics mine). We are not saved *by* good works, but we *do* good works.

In fact, our obligation as believer-priests was spelled out clearly by Jesus when he said that we are to feed the hungry, be a friend to the stranger, provide clothing to those in need, and visit those who are sick and in prison (Matt. 25:31–46). Jesus identified with these people, and he said that failure to minister to *them* is failure to serve him.

This brings us right back to the privilege and responsibility of the priesthood of the believer. Believers can insure the privilege by assuming the responsibility. But as it was with the people of Israel, refusal of the responsibility means loss of the privilege.

Many years ago, I read a statement by the historian Arnold J. Toynbee to the effect that no major nation has been murdered; they all committed suicide. The cycle of nations follows this pattern. A lean, hungry, but hardy people embark upon successful conquest. Then they settle back to enjoy the fruits of conquest. Unknowingly luxurious living saps vitality, and before long that nation falls victim to another lean, hungry, and hardy people. This was true of the Roman Empire. Her legions were invincible. But as the years passed, their enjoyment of the benefits of conquest so sapped their vigor that when the people of central Europe moved in, they found Rome to be little more than an empty shell.

The same thing happens to Christians and groups of Christians. Had the zeal of the first-century Christians remained at a white heat through the centuries, the world would have been evangelized long ago. But tragically, with the passing of time the church began to turn inward and be comfortable. At the same time its missionary zeal waned until, in the New Testament sense, it was practically nonexistent.

Except for an occasional zealous witness, the idea of evangelizing pagan people remained dormant until the late eighteenth century when William Carey followed in the steps of isolated Pietists and ignited a spark that was to become a missionary flame penetrating many previously unreached parts of the world. From that humble start, missionary Carey became known as the father of the modern Protestant missionary movement. And, by 1824, he had supervised six complete and twenty-four partial translations of the Bible.

In these closing days of the twentieth century, we are witnessing mighty movements of spiritual power in spite of the apathy that characterizes many so-called Christian countries. There are vigorous signs of spiritual awakening in many of the Third World countries. A great revival is going on in South Korea. Recently a missionary to Korea told me that Korean Christians are saying that the gospel spread westward from Jerusalem. Now it has come to them. It is their purpose now to take it back to Jerusalem.

Thrilling stories of spiritual vigor are coming through from China and Southeast Asia. And we are beginning to hear about the growing Christian witness in Russia, Poland, and other eastern European countries. Of this we can be sure, whenever and wherever God's people take seriously the responsibility inherent in the principle of the priesthood of the believer, revival will be the result.

Now I want to return to the metaphor of a relay race. The writer of Hebrews, after speaking of the great "cloud of witnesses" who have successfully run their segment of the race, says, "Let *us* run with patience the race that is set before *us*" (Heb. 12:1, italics mine). The word "patience" speaks of that quality which enables us to overcome *all* obstacles and go on to victory. But there is more, for we are told to keep our eyes on "Jesus the author [pioneer] and finisher [goal] of our faith" (Heb. 12:2).

It is this Jesus who is our example and enabler. We run, not for the plaudits of the crowd, but for him who placed us in the race and who made us kings and priests in his cause.

Yes, the race is demanding, but it is rewarding. And the greatest reward of all will be to hear the commendation of Christ whose we are and whom we serve as believer-priests.

Notes

Chapter 1

1. E. Y. Mullins, *The Axioms of Religion* (Philadelphia: American Baptist Publishing Society, 1908), 50. See Herschel H. Hobbs and E. Y. Mullins, *The Axioms of Religion,* rev. ed. (Nashville: Broadman Press, 1978), 47.
2. Ibid., 47.
3. Ibid., 77.
4. Hobbs and Mullins, *Axioms,* 48–50.
5. Ibid., 49.

Chapter 2

1. John D. W. Watts, *Studying the Book of Amos* (Nashville: Broadman Press, 1966), 70.
2. A. T. Robertson, *A Harmony of the Gospels* (Nashville: Broadman Press, 1950), 160.
3. Walter B. Shurden, *The Priesthood of Believers* (Nashville: Convention Press, 1987), 32–33.
4. Hobbs and Mullins, *Axioms,* 30.
5. Robert A. Baker, *A Summary of Christian History* (Nashville: Broadman Press, 1959), 74.
6. Ibid.
7. Hobbs and Mullins, *Axioms,* 30–32; Robert A. Baker, *The Baptist March in History* (Nashville: Convention Press, 1958), 13–26.
8. Timothy George, *Theology of the Reformers* (Nashville: Broadman Press, 1988), 22.
9. Ibid., preface.
10. Ibid., 51, 95, 96.
11. Ibid., 96.
12. Ibid., 97.
13. Ibid., 97.
14. H. Leon McBeth, *The Baptist Heritage* (Nashville: Broadman Press, 1987), 62–63.
15. Frank Mead, *The Baptists* (Nashville: Broadman Press, 1954), 4.

Chapter 3

1. Hobbs and Mullins, *Axioms,* 75.
2. A. T. Robertson, *Word Pictures in the New Testament* (Nashville: Broadman press, 1933), 65–66.
3. A. T. Robertson, *Ward Pictures,* 158–159.

4. Ibid., 159.
5. Herschel H. Hobbs, *Hebrews* (Nashville: Broadman Press, 1979).
6. W. H. Griffith Thomas, *Let Us Go On* (Grand Rapids: Zondervan Publishing House, 1954), .

Chapter 5

1. *Dictionary of the Bible*, James Hastings (New York: Charles Scribner's Sons, 1954), 949.
2. "The Holy Spirit in the Old Testament," *Review and Expositor*, 63 (Spring, 1966), 129.
3. B. H. Carroll, *The Holy Spirit* (Grand Rapids: Zondervan Publishing House, 1939), 17.
4. Herschel H. Hobbs, *The Holy Spirit: Believer's Guide* (Nashville: Broadman Press, 1967), 93–104.
5. Herschel H. Hobbs, *Preaching Values from the Papyri* (Grand Rapids: Baker Book House, 1964), 31.

Chapter 6

1. Hobbs, *Hebrews*, .
2. *Word Pictures in the New Testament* (Nashville: Broadman Press, 1932).
3. Op. Cit., 3:3.

Chapter 7

1. Hobbs and Mullins, *Axioms*, 92.
2. Ibid., 91–109.
3. Herschel H. Hobbs, *The Broadman Bible Commentary* (Nashville: Broadman Press, 1971), 11:268.
4. *The Interpreter's Bible* (New York: Abingdon Press, 1955, 263) lists several uses of the verbal and noun forms (Joel 3:14; Eccles. 40:13; Luke 4:37; 21:25; 1 Cor. 13:1; Heb. 12:19).
5. G. F. Maclear, *A Class-Book of New Testament History* (London: Macmillan and Company, 1932), 69.
6. Charles B. Williams, *The New Testament* (Chicago: Moody Press, 1949), .
7. William F. Arndt and F. Wilbur Gingrich, *A Greek-English Lexicon of the New Testament* (Cambridge: Cambridge University Press, 1957), 644–45.
8. *The New Westminster Dictionary of the Bible*, ed. by Henry Snyder Gehman (Philadelphia: The Westminster Press, 1970), 256.
9. Two of the best manuscripts omit *episkopeō*. But v. 3 may apply just as well to the verb for "tending as a shepherd."
10. Presnall H. Wood, *The Baptist Standard*, 22 June 1988, 6.
11. William H. Lumpkin, *Baptist Confessions of Faith* (Philadelphia: Judson Press, 1959).
12. Herschel H. Hobbs, *The Baptist Faith and Message* (Nashville: Convention Press, 1971), 1–5.

Chapter 8

1. Baker, *A Summary of Christian History*, 15.
2. Ibid., 15.
3. Ibid., 15–23.
4. The above analysis summarizes Baker's treatment, Ibid., 16–25.
5. *The International Standard Bible Encyclopaedia* (Grand Rapids: Eerdman 5).
6. Ibid., 2327.
7. This is a synopsis of Baker, *A Summary of Christian History*, 23–25.
8. Ibid., 132.
9. Ibid., 230–244.
10. Ibid., 235.
11. Reprinted in *The Baptist Standard* (Dallas: Oct. 1981), 3.
12. Ibid., 2.
13. Hobbs and Mullins, *Axioms*, 128.
14. Baker, 267.
15. Ibid., 269–70.
16. Ibid., 272–73.
17. Baker, 350.
18. Mead, *Op. Cit.*, 32–33.
19. Ibid., 36.
20. Ibid., 31.

Chapter 9

1. Robertson, 4:456.
2. Herschel H. Hobbs, *Romans* (Waco, TX: Word Books, 1977), 147.
3. Ibid., 148.
4. B. B. McKinney, *Baptist Hymnal* (Nashville: Broadman Press, 1972), 254.
5. Hobbs, *Romans*, 149.